FOR THE GROOM COLIN COWIE

FOR THE GROOM COLIN COWIE

A Blueprint for a Gentleman's Lifestyle

Text by Jean T. Barrett

DELACORTE PRESS

Introduction

Most people still believe that when it comes to weddings, the groom's responsibilities are to purchase the rings, wear a tuxedo, and show up for the ceremony on time. In actuality today's trends are much more exciting. Getting married isn't just about showing up on time. It is about creating a celebration that is both unique and personal, and the only way to achieve that is for you, the groom, to get involved by expressing your personality in the choices facing you and your bride as you make plans for your wedding.

Think about yourself and your opinions, your likes and your dislikes. You know exactly what kind of car you want to own, what sort of watch you want to wear, which team stands the best chance of winning the Super Bowl, and in what restaurant you want to dine. Why shouldn't your wedding reflect your preferences and sense of style?

I am sure you have a favorite color and a favorite food. I am sure you have an opinion on who should be in the wedding party. I am sure you have a point of view on the type of ceremony to have and on the vows to exchange with your bride. I am sure you have a preference for the wine you would like to serve at your wedding dinner. I am sure you have an opinion on the guest list. I am sure you would like a say on who is seated at your table during the reception. I am sure you have an opinion on the type of music that is played. I am certain you do not want a wedding with bales of lace, tulle, and lots of frou-frou. I am positive you don't want to have to do something at your wedding that makes you feel corny or stupid. With all due respect, I don't think you want a wedding designed by your fiancée's mom!

I have worked on dozens of weddings and personally observed up close how men react toward their role of groom. To many men the wedding is something that women "do" to them; they are clueless about all the arrangements, and the entire experience seems to pass them by. More and more often, however, I am dealing with grooms who know what they want and are determined to have a party that fits their style. Since you have made the single biggest decision in your life–to spend the rest of your days with someone you love–this is a great opportunity to work together and share responsibilities.

Your wedding should reflect your opinions and style on an equal basis with your bride's. I always compare designing a wedding to producing a small movie. It's a complex task that succeeds with strong preproduction work, bringing in the right "cast," and providing good direction. By planning your wedding with your bride, you have a chance to express your statement of style together as a couple, working side by side as coproducers. Your wedding provides a unique opportunity for you as a couple to learn how to work as a team and compromise for each other's benefit. These are skills that will be needed throughout your marriage. By getting involved in the production of your wedding, you won't come in as an extra at the last minute and be told, "You–the groom–stand over there!"

Chances are this is the first time you've noticed, but weddings have changed tremendously over the past decade. It used to be that the rules for a wedding were cast in bronze. The groom wore formal attire. The ceremony followed a traditional format and was generally held in a church or synagogue. An endless receiving line followed the ceremony. The dinner featured a choice of rubber chicken or overcooked beef. The bride's family footed the bill, and the happy couple disappeared immediately after the bouquet toss, to return two weeks later from an expensive honeymoon paid for by the groom.

Many of these traditions still exist, but they are no longer the only model. There are countless possibilities for weddings. The brides and grooms I have worked with are often older and have established their own lifestyles. Frequently the engaged couple is not dependent on their parents to pick up the tab for such a major event. In many cases the mother of the bride is no longer involved in the wedding planning; she gets to enjoy herself, like the other guests. Even when the families of the bride and groom are paying for the wedding, there's an openness to incorporating elements that are important and meaningful to the bride and groom.

Best of all, more and more grooms are involved in everything from deciding on the date and location, to hiring the wedding planner/coordinator, working on the guest list, choosing the menu, music, champagne, and cigars, and determining who pays for what!

This book is written to inspire you in creating new trends, new rituals, and new traditions that paint a personal picture to each and every one of your guests, letting them know who you are as a couple, and sharing what you enjoy in life. I urge you to make the most of your wedding and this opportunity to enhance your relationships with the bride's family, your friends, each other's relatives, and of course, your fiancée. Marriage represents a major life change, and a wedding is a once-in-a-lifetime opportunity to celebrate a transition in a personal and memorable way. A wedding is an occasion to host a fabulous party and make a statement of style to your new family, friends, and loved ones. Think about doing something that is going to be unique and personal, which lets your guest know more about you and your bride.

There are no rules carved in stone except that style must prevail in everything you do. Not only is the focus of attention on you and your bride; this is the opportunity for the two of you to really shine for the first time as the quintessential host and hostess. Think carefully about the menu, how your guests will be entertained, and the importance of being with your closest family members and friends. I defined style in my book, *Weddings*, as a sense of self, a confidence and graciousness evident to everyone with whom you come into contact. Having personal style means knowing yourself, what works for you and what doesn't. True style relates to how we treat one another as human beings. It means behaving with consideration and respect toward others at all times. On your wedding day, acting with true style means creating a personal environment for sharing time with the people who are closest to you, and making each guest as welcome and comfortable as possible.

Every couple should take the time and design a unique wedding that personifies who they really are. In these pages are my ideas for you to consider in every aspect of your wedding, from the proposal to honeymoon destinations.

Getting married is more than just saying "I do" at the wedding. This book is about being a gentleman in the truest sense of the word, from understanding how to be a host to learning the myriad of ways a couple can keep romance and passion in their day-to-day life.

Good luck, be creative, and have fun in the process!

Best wishes,

Colin

A note: Many of the readers of this book are men engaged to be married. Many others are in a serious relationship and considering their options. Some are newlyweds. Thus, when we refer at various places to your girlfriend, fiancée, future wife, or wife, we use the terms interchangeably to mean the woman with whom you are having a serious relationship.

Chapter 1

Treating a Woman Like a Lady

What Do Women Really Want?

A fter reading this chapter title, you probably intend to skip directly to the next chapter, because you believe you already know how to treat a lady. And if you are reading this book, you most likely are in a serious relationship and may even be engaged. So does that prove you know how to treat women?

Maybe so. Perhaps you are a master of the masculine art of coddling your lady love. Perhaps she is constantly gushing about you to her girlfriends, reporting on the latest courtly compliment you paid her, the romantic bouquet of roses that arrived unexpectedly at her place of business, the gourmet dinner you prepared for her the other evening.

Or maybe we might review just what it is, to cite Freud, that women want.

Women want to be taken care of, the same as men do. And in this age of liberated women, this statement might seem like the height of political incorrectness. Your own girlfriend might deny it strenuously. But I insist it's true. It's human nature.

It's not that women want to be kept, or have decisions made for them, or in any way to abdicate their natural powers and abilities. But they do want the man in their life to take care of them, to do things for them, to constantly remind them how special they are. They may never tell you that. You're supposed to know.

Now that things are serious with you and your girlfriend, you may want to consider a little behavior modification. This chapter is filled with suggestions on how you can do those little things that will forever endear you to her.

The Art of the Compliment

Women love compliments–as do we all. Everyone wants to be recognized for their accomplishments, major and minor. It's important to make sure the person in your life knows you love everything about her–her ability to pull together a huge proposal before an impossible deadline, her masterful way with a hollandaise sauce, and how gorgeous she looks when you're ready to head out for a special night on the town. Compliments about her appearance are especially appreciated. Most men are notorious for not noticing important things like how their girlfriends, fiancées, and wives look. At least most men don't mention it.

Whenever you dispense compliments, be very, very careful not to be generic with a "one size fits all" comment. For example, "you look nice" doesn't mean anything. Instead, look for those fine details that demonstrate you are a man of discernment and taste, that you can differentiate between the ordinary and the exceptional. Specificity is key to the masterful compliment.

Rather than telling her that her hair looks "nice," pick a detail that has captured your attention. "Your hair has beautiful highlights," "That haircut you just got really brings out your eyes," and "I love the way your hair curls around your ears" are much more compelling than the word *nice*.

Suppose you like the dress she is wearing. It's not enough to say you like the dress. It's what she brings to the dress that is important. You want to say something like, "That dress looks gorgeous on you," or even "With your light skin the color of that dress is truly stunning."

Got the idea? You should be delivering compliments to your girlfriend on a regular basis, and you should mean them with all sincerity.

Being Romantic

Couples who are engaged and newlyweds often begin their lives together thinking that marriage is easy and blissful, that life is effortless when you're in love, and that getting to know each other is such fun. It doesn't seem as though you could ever tire of such a wonderful person.

But keeping romance in your relationship takes effort. It's something that both husband and wife need to work at constantly in order to enjoy the rewards. A long, happy marriage doesn't just happen. It requires constant maintenance and energy.

I always compare marriage to a garden. If you tend to it, removing problems like weeds, and provide the plants plenty of water and nutrients, you will probably have fruitful results. If you neglect it, the garden will probably wither or go dormant and could die. It's the same with a marriage or any long-term relationship. It's important to keep the lines of communication open at all times. You have to be able to express your feelings of insecurity and anxiety as well as your feelings of love, tenderness, and commitment. You must bring up issues that are bothering you and if you sense that something is bothering your fiancée or wife, express your concern and ask if there's a problem.

Remember that romance isn't just for Valentine's Day, birthdays, and holidays. You can keep romance in your marriage by showing your wife that you're thinking of her when she's least expecting it. Maybe she's had a difficult week at the office, the kids have been driving her crazy, she's not feeling well, she's having a problem with a family member or friend, or you just intuitively sense that she's depressed about something. A great way to lift her spirits is to send her flowers, for no reason at all, and of course include a personally written note reassuring her of your love and support: "I wanted you to know I was thinking of you today and love you very much. I'll see you at seven for dinner. Love, Paul." If you have a florist whom you often use, send over a dozen of your personal note cards so that you can dictate messages over the telephone that will be delivered with the flowers.

Having flowers arrive out of the blue with a personalized note is a great surprise with more impact than carrying a bouquet home.

How to Find a Good Florist

Gorgeous flowers are indispensable to my business, and I have long-standing relationships with many extremely talented, dependable floral professionals. If you are looking for a good local florist, ask friends who entertain if they have a recommendation. Also, when you attend social or business events, notice if the floral arrangements seem particularly attractive, and ask the event organizer for the name of the florist who provided them. If you are in a strange city, ask the concierge of the best hotel in town to recommend a florist–although be cautious if he recommends an in-hotel supplier.

Spending what is frequently referred to as "quality time" with your partner is another practice that will serve you well in marriage. Many of my friends in healthy relationships enjoy a regularly scheduled "date night." Once a week they schedule an evening together, have a leisurely meal, and enjoy each other's company. Without specifically setting aside time to spend relating to each other, many couples' lives would be a round of board meetings, scheduled commitments, and social obligations with other people. It's amazing how quickly you can fall into a routine that leaves little time for each other.

I also encourage men who are getting married to practice doing special things for their wives-to-be on a daily basis–small favors, quick chores, little things that you can easily do but that will mean the world to her, making her feel pampered. Give her a surprise breakfast in bed one Sunday morning. If she comes home late from work, have a pitcher of martinis chilling and her favorite Chinese take-out ready. Buy some scented body oil and learn how to give her a back massage or, even better, a foot massage. Take her car in to be washed and waxed. These little favors cost you just a bit of time, but they mean so much. It's the kind of thing that can help sustain a loving relationship over time. It may even make you irreplaceable.

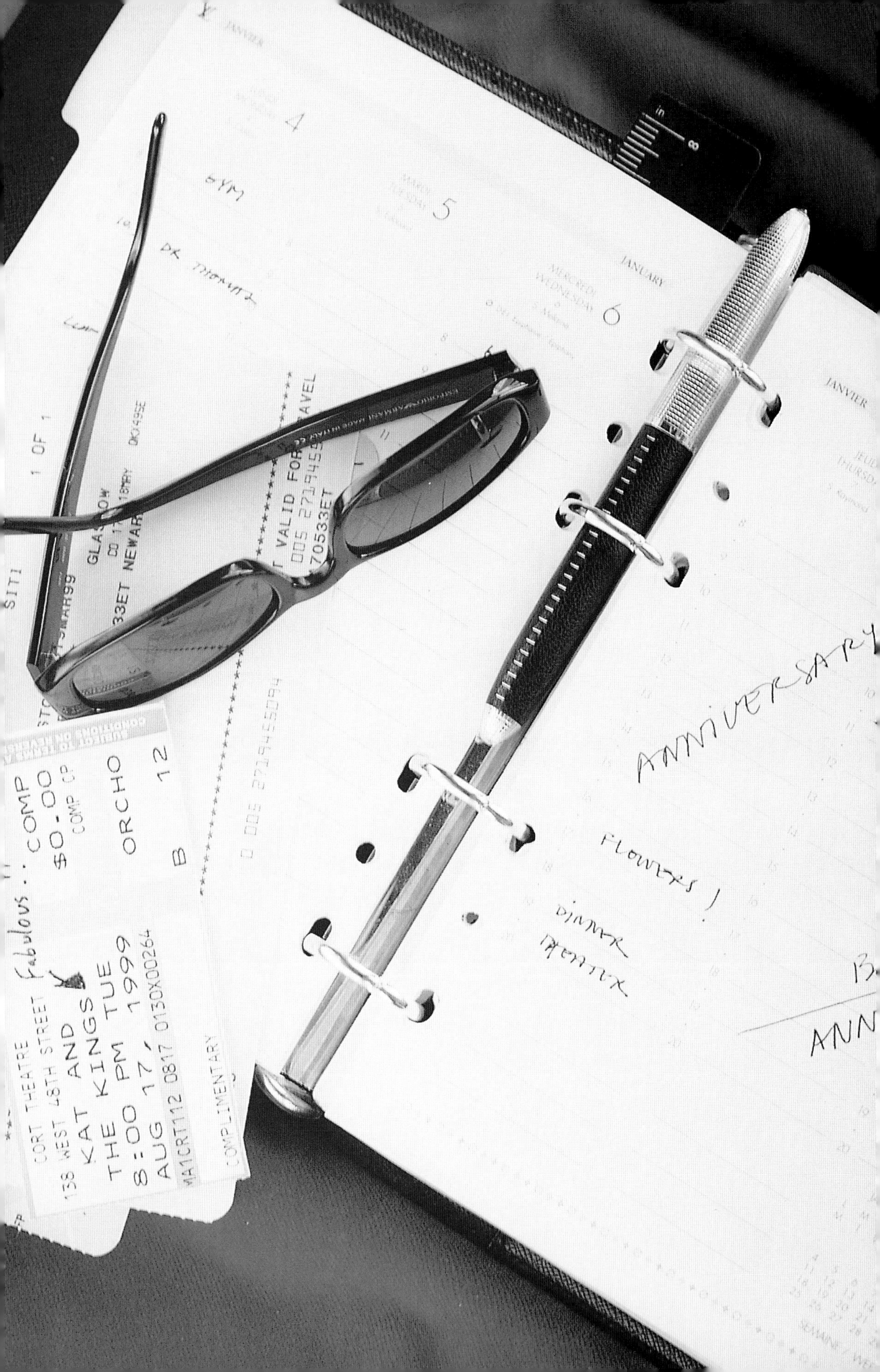
CORT THEATRE
138 WEST 48TH STREET
KAT AND THE KINGS
THE PM TUE
8:00
AUG 17, 1999
COMP
$0.00
ORCHO
COMPLIMENTARY
JANUARY
WEDNESDAY 6
ANNIVERSARY
FLOWERS!
DINNER

Chapter 2

Being a Gentleman

I suggest you take a long, hard look at yourself. Are you in need of some major adjustments or minor adjustments?

Your wedding represents a great opportunity to begin retooling and refining your image, if it needs it. Marriage is a turning point in a man's life. Things will be different after your wedding since you will no longer be dealing with the world as a single person, but as a couple. This is one of those turning points in life when you can decide how you want to be perceived, and you have the opportunity to make the changes that may be necessary.

Think of how you appear to others. Consider the people you respect and admire and, conversely, those who have always disappointed you. What type of person do you want to be? Are you going to be a macho guy with no social graces, a man who does exactly as he pleases without a thought about the feelings of others? Or do you want to be a gentleman that people admire, one who is courteous of others and treats others, especially his wife, with love and respect?

I am on a mission to bring back the art of being a gentleman. When I grew up in South Africa, it was expected that I treat others with deference and respect. If my mother or another lady entered the room, I rose to my feet. I was taught to introduce myself to others in a friendly, gracious manner. At school and at home, I was required to write thank-you notes when I received a gift or when I had been invited to a friend's home. It was expected that I would write a letter of condolence if someone I knew passed on. These rules of behavior, which by adolescence were firmly ingrained in my persona, have remained with me to this day. I have long been thankful to my parents and schooling for instilling in me a sense of proper conduct that guides me in both social and business relationships.

When I first moved to the United States and began my dealings in the business world, I was in for a rude awakening. I was amazed at the lack of common courtesy I found in the people I dealt with. Granted, this was the 1980s—a time when many people had suddenly made huge amounts of money and because they were so wealthy, they felt that the rules of social behavior did not apply to them specifically.

As the years have passed, the situation has, if anything, gotten worse. Many men, particularly young men, lack simple good manners. They have little sense of what it means to be gracious, thoughtful, and charming. Because they don't know how to act properly, they come across as rude, boorish, and self-centered. Perhaps they were never taught how to be considerate of others, or maybe they were told but just didn't feel it was important to listen.

I date the decline in gentlemanly behavior to the late 1960s, when the "do your own thing" era dawned. At about the same time feminism began to come to the fore. Early advocates of women's liberation insisted that they wanted no special treatment from the male gender–no doors held open, no standing when a woman entered the room, no "ladies first." What used to be "good manners" was offensive to many women, who saw it as patronizing. Men got the message and responded accordingly. Over the decades, as America experienced the Vietnam War, Woodstock, marijuana, Watergate, the disco era, and the excesses of the 1980s, we also threw good manners out the window.

When I talk about having good manners, I don't mean the rules that fill etiquette books–although many of those still make good sense. Having good manners, to me, is a very basic concept. It means being respectful and considerate toward others. If you behave respectfully toward others, you have good manners. If you are mindful and considerate of others' feelings, you have good manners.

For me, one of the icons of good manners is a gentleman named Frank Bowling. Frank is general manager of the Hotel Bel-Air in Los Angeles, which is considered by many to be the best hotel in the world. Indeed, Frank is perhaps the ultimate gentleman of our time, as he is always gracious, always polite, and always impeccably well dressed. Frank is a master of the prompt, cordial thank-you note. He interfaces with thousands of people during the course of a year, and I have never heard him speak ill of anyone or anyone speak ill of him. His presence has enhanced the Bel-Air's reputation as the most sought-after destination for travelers from all over the world. He sets an example for his staff, who are among the best-trained and most polite hotel employees I have ever encountered.

I ran into Frank at the hotel the other day and asked him, "What would you say is the most important quality for a gentleman to have?" He thought for just a second. "Sensitivity," he replied. Of course, he was right on the money. Being sensitive to others at all times is certainly the essence of a true gentleman.

How does sensitivity, this idea of being a gentleman, translate to the real world? Here are a few examples. You're at a friend's party, and you see a guest standing alone. Perhaps you walk over to the person, break the ice with a conversational opener, and introduce yourself. The person, who may not know anyone at the party, will probably be delighted at your friendliness, and you just may have a great chat. Or perhaps you're on a plane and see an elderly person struggling with a heavy carry-on bag. I've been on flights where I've watched rows of strong young men ignore another passenger trying to stow her luggage in the overhead bin. Step up, politely ask if you can give her a hand, and then do it. The warm feeling you'll get from doing the right thing will last half the flight.

Let's get a bit more practical. A gentleman rinses off the bathroom sink after shaving. He removes stray hair from the drain after showering. He puts the toilet seat down after he is finished. If his aim is a bit off, he wipes the bowl clean with tissue paper. These practices are all about being sensitive to others in your life.

Behaving like a gentleman is easy, once you have the mind-set. It's a matter of combining sensitivity with respect and courtesy toward others. If that sounds like a tall order, try to keep in mind the image

The Importance of Good Manners While Dining

It is easy to see how people were brought up by watching them at a dining table. Does the man sit up straight, with elbows at his side and utensils set neatly on the plate? Or does he slouch, gesticulating with the knife as he jabs a fork into a slab of steak and stuffs it into his mouth? The saying is "You are what you eat." I think *how* you eat says more about you than *what* you eat. If you are unsure whether your habits need modification, set up a mirror and watch yourself eat breakfast or lunch sometime; I guarantee you will immediately see yourself from another diner's point of view, and you may want to make a few changes! If you don't like what you see, chances are no one else will, either.

Here are a few pointers:

Eat quietly. Chew with your mouth closed. Don't slurp when you drink liquids. Eating and drinking should be done as quietly as possible.

The knife is not a pointer. Never gesture with a utensil. If you're not taking food from your plate to your mouth, your utensils shouldn't be in your hands.

Don't load up your fork with large amounts of food. The fork is not a shovel. Take small forkfuls, and eat slowly. You're not in a competition.

When dining buffet style, make several trips to the buffet rather than loading up your plate with huge helpings of food. Fish, meat, and chicken weren't meant to go on the same plate.

Never blow your nose at the table. It's highly unappetizing for other diners. Excuse yourself and walk to the bathroom or a private area.

Unless a babysitter is caring for your children at home or you are a physician on call, there is no excuse ever to have a cell phone at the dinner table. If you need to make

of a gentleman you admire, who always seems to know the right thing to do, even in difficult circumstances. Ask yourself how that person would handle each situation you encounter. You can't change your behavior overnight, but modest changes over time will gradually lead you to an entirely new approach.

Ah, you reply; you are marrying a liberated woman who has no ties to the old-fashioned practices of her parents' generation: holding doors, lighting cigarettes, and so on. I must say I have never in my life met a woman who doesn't appreciate being dealt with respectfully and deferentially. I have never met a woman who doesn't like it when a man stands up as she enters the room, or opens a door for her when getting into a car, or sends her flowers just *because*. Women *are* special; they are different, and they deserve to be treated accordingly. Women should be treated like a precious commodity. I also think that one's parents, friends, children, and even business associates should receive similar courtesies. A little thought goes a long way, and I assure you, the dividends will be returned to you tenfold.

For specifics, here are a few practices that will help set you apart from others of your gender.
A Gentlemen Always ...

Rises when a woman enters the room.

Rises, or pulls himself up slightly as a mark of courtesy, when a woman leaves a table.

Pulls out the chair for a lady when she is being seated.

Walks around the car and opens the door for a lady or elderly person.

Walks on the side next to the traffic when he is with a lady.

Stands up when introduced to someone, and extends a firm handshake.

Knows how to make a proper introduction, speaking each person's name distinctly and introducing first the younger person to the older and the man to the woman, as a mark of deference.

Lets a woman precede him through a door and holds the door for her.

Lights a woman's cigarette.

Serves the ladies first at dinner, then the men.

Is careful not to use profanity.

Is always punctual, or apologizes in advance if an emergency has arisen that makes him late. Always telephones to alert others that he has been detained.

Is a good conversationalist who asks other people about themselves and their interests rather than babbling on about himself.

Sends flowers, chocolates, or gifts to the woman in his life, often for no reason at all.

Is shaved and well groomed, with clean nails and neatly trimmed hair.

Dresses appropriately, knowing when to wear a jacket, when to add a tie, when to be casual.

Wears clean and well-polished shoes, and clean, well-pressed shirts and trousers.

Sends prompt thanks via fax, email, or hand-written notes.

an urgent call during dinner, excuse yourself and walk to another room to place the call.

Never come to the table with dirty hands or nails. There's nothing worse than noticing someone's filthy nails while you're eating.

If you have dietary restrictions or preferences that you have not communicated to your host, don't make a fuss if the food served doesn't fit within your diet. Simply tell the host that you're sorry, but you don't eat that dish and ask for a larger portion of the other selections if possible.

Never talk with food in your mouth.

Never interrupt others or try to talk over other guests' conversations.

Don't reach past your neighbor to get something on the table; ask for it to be passed to you.

When you have finished eating, place your utensils parallel to each other across your plate, with the knife blade and fork tines resting close to the plate's center so the plate may be easily removed by the server.

Chapter 3

The Proposal

The decision to ask someone to be your bride is probably the single most important decision you will ever make. Deciding that you are prepared to spend the rest of your life with one particular person is a turning point in life. It's just as important to your girlfriend as it is to you, so spend some time on making your marriage proposal personal, creative, meaningful, and memorable. Plan it carefully, and infuse it with the style and meaning it deserves. It's a moment that will stay with your fiancée forever. Every woman I know remembers every single detail of her marriage proposal. Make it a good memory that she will cherish forever.

Don't be like the husband of a dear friend of mine. When I began this book, I asked a number of friends about their proposals. One woman told me, "Oh, I had the most romantic one"–her voice dripped with sarcasm. Her husband-to-be was in the supermarket with her late one weeknight after a long day at their respective offices. They were standing in front of the produce department, bathed in the neon lights, looking at the cabbages. Suddenly he pulled out a ring, and she said, "What's that?" And he said, "Well, you know, you wanted to." And she said, "I wanted to what?" He said, "You know." She said, "It's not like that, you have to ask me." So he asked, "Well, do you?" And she said, "No, you have to ask me out fully." Finally he was able to choke out, "Will you marry me?" She said, "No, you have to get down on your knees." So he knelt down in the middle of the produce department, reached out for her hand, and proposed. She accepted–but believe me, she's never let him forget the incident!

Even though that approach was memorable, it is not one I highly recommend.

It's All in the Timing

In researching this book, I had a great deal of fun polling my female friends to learn how they were proposed to. But my questions turned up a real surprise. I was astonished to learn that many of the women I know did not experience the traditional, down-on-his-knees, romantic proposal. Instead, these women took matters into their own hands. They issued The Ultimatum.

The Ultimatum–two words that strike terror in every man's heart. Here you are: You think everything's going well. You're in love with a wonderful woman. Your relationship is progressing steadily. But you're just not quite ready to pop the question.

She, on the other hand, is losing patience. She's wondering if you're serious, if you'll ever settle down. She's questioning the relationship. Her friends and family are asking leading questions. Her self-esteem is taking a beating. Finally something gives. She issues The Ultimatum.

The Ultimatum takes a variety of forms, but it usually includes a threat to leave unless a ring is produced, pronto. Women don't like having to set a deadline for a marriage proposal. It can feel demeaning and often leads to tearful confrontations. On the receiving end many men, understandably, feel defensive and trapped. Often they'll protest, "But I was going to ask you"–which, to the woman, is too little, too late.

All in all The Ultimatum is no fun for either party. It has the ability to make or break a good thing. While many marriages that resulted from ultimatums are lasting, wonderful unions, I don't think it's a very romantic way to start a lifelong commitment. And I don't think you want her to remember your marriage proposal as a response to an ultimatum.

This leads to the important issue of timing. You certainly need to consider when to propose, and you may need to think about it before you feel completely ready. Timing your proposal is a delicate matter. Wait too long, and you'll find yourself on the receiving end of The Ultimatum. Jump the gun, or time your proposal awkwardly, and you risk being turned down like a bedspread.

Ultimately you'll have to decide when the best time is for you to propose. Take a couple of factors into consideration. First, I suggest proposing on a calendar date that has significance to your fiancée-to-be. Perhaps an important anniversary in your relationship is coming up–an anniversary of your first meeting or your first date. Perhaps her birthday is right around the corner. Maybe there is a time of year that has particular appeal to you and your girlfriend. The holiday season, with its emphasis on celebrating, giving gifts, and getting together with family and friends, is a great time to become engaged. One bride related to me her husband's unforgettable proposal as he knelt down in front of the tree their first Christmas together. "Christmas is my favorite time of year, and I had never shared a tree with anyone else, so it was incredibly meaningful," she recalls. As she looked at one of the branches of the tree, a sparkling ring was tied to the branch with a piece of white ribbon, on which was written in gold script, "I love you–will you marry me?"

And trust me: Every woman who is involved in a serious relationship can't help but wonder, as Valentine's Day approaches, whether she will receive more than a bouquet of roses or a box of chocolates.

But maybe Valentine's Day is too predictable for you. One of my friends told me that February 14 was the one-year anniversary of the first date with her husband. He gave her the traditional flowers on the day itself but invited her to a dinner at his condo the following evening. On the table was a lush bouquet of long-stemmed red roses. On the stem of one of the roses was a sparkling diamond engagement ring. Because my friend wasn't expecting anything, her fiancé-to-be had to keep drawing her attention to the flowers. "Look how beautiful they are, honey," he'd beg. When she finally noticed the ring, she was incredibly excited and happy, partly because it was such a surprise.

Another option is a private New Year's Eve party, just for the two of you. Only you will know that as the minutes tick off to midnight, you have a surprise in store for her.

A Proposal She Can't Refuse

Entire books have been written on the myriad of unique ways that men (and sometimes women) propose marriage. These range from traditional to outrageous. Whatever you choose to do, your marriage proposal should fit your style. Don't feel obliged to hire a plane to write your proposal in the sky—unless your girlfriend is an air traffic controller! You need to think about which approach suits your style, and what would most please your future fiancée. Keep in mind that nearly all women have a soft spot for romance. She may be a successful, high-powered executive by day, but when it comes to a proposal of marriage, you'd be amazed how an old-fashioned, gentlemanly, romantic approach works best.

First, consider the setting for your proposal. What environment is right—your favorite restaurant, a cabin in the mountains, a secluded beach, a carriage ride in the park? Perhaps you and your girlfriend have wonderful memories of a favorite restaurant. What could be more appropriate than proposing there? Enlist a trusted maître d' as your coconspirator, and arrange for a romantic dinner for two. At the right moment between dinner and dessert, a discreet signal from you sends the waiter over with a little box on a silver tray, along with a handwritten note. When your girlfriend opens the note, she'll read a heartfelt letter from you expressing your love and wish to marry her. Inside the box a glittering diamond is ready to be mounted in the setting of her choice. What could be more romantic and memorable?

Friends of mine who had been dating for quite some time went to dinner at their favorite Chinese restaurant. They relaxed over a delicious meal, and when he asked for the bill, it was presented along with a pair of the customary fortune cookies. She opened hers and was astonished to find that the cookie contained a beautiful ruby and diamond ring, and instead of a fortune, there was a small strip of paper reading, "Will you marry me?" She immediately accepted. (In case you're wondering, my clever friend obtained fortune cookies in advance, carefully broke one in half to insert the ring and the proposal "fortune," then glued the halves back together so that the break was virtually undetectable. The waiter was instructed to place the reconstructed cookie close to the lady as he set it down on the table, so that she would reach for it first.)

Maybe you love taking mountain hikes together. Plan an all-day hike on a beautiful day. Do some advance work and find a resting place on the trail that's relatively private. When you reach your resting spot, put down your backpack and whip out a chilled half bottle of champagne and two champagne flutes. Pour her a bit of bubbly, then tell her what's on your mind.

If you enjoy cooking, I can't think of a better way to show your affection than by creating a special dinner that culminates in asking for her hand in marriage. Light dozens of candles to create a romantic mood; play her favorite music; serve her favorite wines; and fill the menu with her best-loved foods. It makes a great setting for romance and demonstrates your thoughtfulness and commitment.

When professional football player Rodney Peete decided to propose to actress Holly Robinson, he wanted it to be an occasion she'd never forget. So he conspired with Holly's mother, agent Dolores Robinson, to arrange a surprise on the set of Holly's TV show, *Hangin' with Mr. Cooper*. During a routine taping of the show, Holly's character had to open a door on the set. When she did, instead of one of the actors on the show, there was Rodney, handsomely attired in a suit and tie. He dropped to one knee, pulled a velvet-covered box out of his pocket, and asked, "Holly, will you marry me?" Holly was only too delighted to say yes, and since the cameras kept rolling, the couple has the videotape of their proposal as a keepsake.

One of my favorite proposal stories was told to me by Dayna Steele, the Houston-based radio talk show host, who is married to NASA research pilot Dr. Charlie Justiz. In the early 1990s Dayna was moving into a house with Charlie, who worked on the space program and was close friends with astronaut Colonel Tom Henricks, USAF. During the move Dayna accidentally came across what she immediately knew was her engagement ring, but nothing had been said, so she put it away and tried not to think about it. But she wondered as the months passed and there was no proposal. One day she realized what Charlie had planned: he was going to get his astronaut friend to take the ring on the space shuttle! Sure enough, the launch of space shuttle *Atlantis* was scheduled in November, 1991, and Colonel Henricks had the diamond engagement ring on his little finger under his orange space suit. (He later told Dayna that he took it off and put it away as soon as they were weightless because he was scared to death it would float off and be lost!)

But the story isn't over; the shuttle returned, and still no proposal from Charlie. Then just before Christmas that same year, Dayna and Charlie were attending a holiday performance. After the show they went backstage to congratulate the actors. Dayna was totally astonished when the two performers proposed to her on Charlie's behalf. As Dayna said, "Two actors who had spent most of the evening in drag were possibly the last people in the world I was expecting a proposal from! Charlie had pulled it off—he surprised me!" Charlie then presented Dayna with the much-traveled ring, which had been engraved, "109 times around the world for you. Flown on STS-44, 12/91 Love, Cisco." (Cisco is Charlie's tactical call sign when flying.)

Some men will go to great the lengths to propose. Here are some ideas to start you thinking creatively about how to propose to your future wife.

• Take her for a weekend ski trip. When you return to the lodge after a day out on the slopes, make sure the hot tub in your room is bubbling and a bottle of champagne is on ice. After the relaxing hot tub, arrange for room service to deliver a private dinner for two. Under the silver cover that she thinks is protecting her favorite chocolate dessert, insert a tiny box. The rest is up to you.

• Arrange for a night on the town, complete with chauffeur-driven limousine, a night of theater, and a late dinner at a romantic spot, followed by dancing. As she settles back into the limo after the festivities, take her hand and say, "There's only one thing that could make this evening more special." "What's

that?" she'll respond. You answer, "If you will agree to be my wife."

• What about proposing on a plane? I don't recommend doing this unless you're in first class, since there's no space or privacy in coach, and the flight attendants are too busy to assist. But if you are in first class, here's one scenario. Before the meal is served, you disappear for a few minutes. While you're gone, the flight attendant appears with a bottle of champagne and fills your girlfriend's glass. Then the attendant suggests that she watch a particular channel on the individual video screens. There you are on screen, in a video that you prepared earlier. Talking right to your girlfriend, you explain how important the relationship is to you and how you want to spend the rest of your life with her. As the video ends, the real you appears in the aisle and kneels to propose.

• I think one of the most romantic spots for a proposal is a secluded beach, perhaps at a quiet time of day, such as early morning or dusk. Take your girlfriend for a quiet sunset walk on the beach. You can lead the conversation to your plans for the future and your feelings for her. Afterward you can dine at a restaurant nearby and celebrate into the evening.

• A man I know concocted an elaborately scripted treasure hunt for his girlfriend. There were at least a dozen clues, each of which made humorous reference to an experience they had together. The clues took the girlfriend through her own home, then to her gym, to a friend's home, and finally to his house, where a series of three clues led her to an antique sideboard in his living room. (He shepherded her the entire way.) In the sideboard was a little velvet jewelry box–you know the rest! She was thrilled, and has since told the story of the great engagement treasure hunt dozens of times.

Words to Win Her Over

A proposal of marriage is not the time for ad-libbing or falling back on clichés. Your words should come right from the heart, but unless you have total confidence in your ability to deliver a crisp and compelling speech that will have your future fiancée melting in your arms, your proposal should be scripted in advance and rehearsed.

Well before you intend to propose, start formulating in your head exactly what you want to say. Don't just blurt out, "Will you marry me?" Instead, lead up to the big question with your thoughts on your relationship, expressions of your love for her, and your hopes and plans for the future. Romance her. Tell her, in your own words, how much you've been thinking about her in the recent weeks and months. Tell her how certain you are about your feelings for her and your future together. Express your feelings of love and your promise to love and care for her from this day onward. Tell her that you would like to spend the rest of your life with her. Your proposal of marriage will be entirely personal, coming straight from your heart.

Meeting the In-Laws

Congratulations! She's accepted your marriage proposal with delight. Now you must face–her parents!

Today it is rare for the man to go through the formality of asking his fiancée's parents for her hand in marriage. But I think it is a custom that deserves resurrection. I feel the groom should make an effort to visit his fiancée's parents and ask for their blessing. It is an act of consideration and respect. Your fiancée's parents raised her, cared for her, doted on her–and probably still do. Your future in-laws may be from an older generation and may have been brought up in a more traditional environment. If your fiancée is still living under the parental roof, the prospect of her engagement is a major change. Her parents deserve to have the news told to them gently and with the utmost respect.

In this day and age you may not feel comfortable literally asking the parents for their daughter's hand in marriage, as the old phrase goes. After all, your fiancée has a mind of her own and makes her own decisions. But there are several ways to handle this in a manner that pays respect to the parents while still keeping your (and your bride's) self-respect intact.

If your fiancée is quite young and still living with her parents, it's very appropriate to ask for a meeting with her father or with both parents to tell them of your love for their daughter, your commitment to care for her, and your plans for the future. This is an opportunity for you to show her parents who you are–that you're responsible, well mannered, kind, and considerate and that you'll take care of their daughter. Her parents will be impressed by your sincerity and reassured that their daughter is marrying a man who knows how things should be done: properly and with consideration.

Perhaps your fiancée is older and has been living on her own for some time. I still think it is important to get off on the right foot with her parents by approaching them formally and asking for their blessing. Particularly if your fiancée is very close to her parents, such a gesture can make all the difference in how her parents perceive you. If you don't feel it is appropriate to meet with her parents by yourself, arrange a dinner for the four of you to get better acquainted. During the dinner you or your fiancée can share your plans, and at the same time you have an opportunity to communicate to them your love for, and commitment to, their daughter.

Speaking with your fiancée's parents doesn't have to be done in person, if you live in different areas of the country or the world. But it should be done personally, with a well-thought-out phone call. Your fiancée could join you on the call as well. After the call is over, it is gracious to write a short letter to the parents reiterating some of the issues you discussed and thanking them for their support.

Marybeth

and

Sudhir

Chapter 4

The Ring

A Symbol of Eternity

When you present your girlfriend with a ring symbolizing your intent to marry, you are part of a tradition that dates back to around 2000 B.C. when Egyptian jewelers crafted elaborate ornaments for the pharaohs. The Egyptians believed that the unending circle of the ring symbolized eternity. Later, during the Roman Empire, men gave women rings forged of iron to publicly affirm their commitment to marry. By the second century A.D., gold was becoming a popular material for wedding rings. In 1477 Archduke Maximilian of Austria was one of the first grooms on record to give a diamond engagement ring to his bride, Mary of Burgundy. That ring had a natural, uncut crystal diamond. It wasn't until the end of the fifteenth century that jewelers first developed rudimentary techniques for cutting facets into diamonds, releasing the brilliance and fire of the gemstone. But diamonds were too rare and expensive for anyone but the nobility to afford.

By the eighteenth century, an early version of the diamond cut we now know as the brilliant was introduced. Around 1870 huge diamond deposits were discovered in Africa, greatly expanding the world's supply of this precious stone. For the first time diamonds were within the reach of affluent buyers, not just the nobility.

In our century, the gemstone-set engagement ring has come into its own. Modern polishing techniques and innovations in cutting gems give buyers more choices than ever before. The wide array of options requires the groom and his bride to do their homework before committing to the purchase of their engagement and wedding rings.

Buying a Jewel: Don't Do It Alone!

We've all seen the clichéd scene in films, where the bridegroom drops to one knee, eloquently proposes marriage, and holds out a tiny jeweler's box in which gleams the perfect engagement ring. That scene plays fine in the movies, but it's not the only approach. To make sure your prospective fiancée is just as thrilled with the engagement ring as you'd like her to be, you might want to consider letting her in on the selection process.

Here's why. You want to get this right the first time. If she's like most women, your future wife will wear her ring twenty-four hours a day, seven days a week, for the rest of her life. She'll do everything with that ring on, and you want her to love it. And frankly, it's simply a modern approach. The practice of secretly buying the ring and springing it on an unsuspecting girl dates from the days when men made all the decisions. That era is long gone, and believe me, your future wife wants a say in what kind of ring goes on her finger. I recommend you consult with her.

Now, it is true that involving your girlfriend in the process of selecting a ring will take away the element of surprise. If that's a concern, there are several approaches you can take. One is to enlist the help of someone who is close to your future fiancée and whose taste you trust. This might be one of her girlfriends, or even her mother if they have a close enough relationship. Take your confidante to the jewelry store and get her advice on rings that will suit your girlfriend's taste.

Another approach is to select the major gemstone for the ring yourself and present it to your fiancée at the time you propose. You'll have to decide on the type and size of the stone, and then the two of you can take the stone to a jeweler and have it set according to her preferences, either as a solitaire or with other stones. This approach allows you to make the lavish gesture of presenting the ring box, while letting your fiancée choose the look and style of the ring. A side benefit to this strategy is that you can maintain control over the cost of the ring by selecting the major stone in advance.

A third tactic is to buy an inexpensive ring as a "stand-in" for the real thing. As you give it to your fiancée, you can explain that you wanted to surprise her, but that you were sure she wanted to pick out her ring with you, so you have set aside time over the weekend to hit the jewelry stores. The ring you're presenting is just a special gift to her as a token of what lies ahead.

Engagement Rings and Wedding Bands

The most traditional style for the engagement ring and wedding band is a diamond solitaire ring (a simple mounting of a single stone) and plain wedding band of platinum or gold. While this style remains extremely popular, there are hundreds of alternatives. Some brides choose to wear only one gemstone ring as a combined engagement ring and wedding band. Others choose a wedding band and engagement ring set that has been designed to fit snugly together and give the appearance of a single piece of jewelry. Some couples forgo the engagement ring for the bride altogether and select matching wedding bands that symbolize their equality in the marriage. A variation on that is to choose matching wedding rings of gold or platinum, hers set with diamonds and his plain.

Women's wedding bands may be utterly plain, or they may have gemstones; whatever the style, the wedding band should complement and enhance the look of the engagement ring. If the engagement ring and wedding band are worn together, as is customary, the engagement ring is worn inside, so as to be "closest to the heart."

Keep in mind that down the road you may wish to buy your wife an "eternity" or "anniversary" ring symbolizing a milestone in your marriage. Eternity rings often feature bands of diamonds and, if worn on the fourth finger of the left hand, should complement the engagement and wedding rings.

A ring style is a matter of taste, although I always advise a conservative, classic approach.

Remember that highly stylized, modern, or fancy jewelry can date very quickly. A trendy setting that you and your bride think is suitable now may look passé in twenty years, while a simple, classic setting will look just as beautiful in the future as it does today.

Don't overlook vintage or heirloom rings. Perhaps there is a ring with a lot of meaning to you that has been passed down in your family. When you propose, you have a wonderful opportunity to explain to your fiancée the history and importance of the ring to you and your relatives, which is a lovely way to welcome her into your family. Or if there is no heirloom ring but you know your fiancée loves vintage jewelry, why not select a beautiful style from an antiquarian jewelry store? An art deco platinum ring from the 1930s, or an understated Tiffany gold band set with emeralds, makes a distinctive yet classic choice for an engagement ring. Because vintage rings have a history and are one-of-a-kind, they can be a wonderful way to express your feelings to your fiancée.

I do not believe it is necessary to give a woman a huge rock as an engagement diamond. The engagement ring is not the place to make a statement of how much money you have to put into a gemstone. Huge gemstones are simply not appropriate for daytime wear out in public. They call attention to themselves and to the woman wearing them. Such attention can even be a security risk for a woman who takes public transportation or who is traveling alone. A large ring is also impractical for many of the activities that your bride may be involved in, such as working out at the gym, rock climbing, or swimming. A ring that she must take off repeatedly is more likely to be lost. Smaller diamond or gemstone rings can be just as beautiful, of exceptional quality, and more practical for the long term.

There will be plenty of opportunities later in life for you to lavish your bride with large jewels. You can buy her a fabulous colored diamond cocktail ring for gala occasions, or a chunky, modern Italian design for less formal events, such as dinner with friends. But the engagement ring should be appropriately sized so that your wife will feel comfortable wearing it all the time, no matter what she's doing or where she's going.

Engraving a message or initials on the inside of the wedding rings is a romantic touch. Many couples like to engrave their initials and the date of their wedding. Others prefer a personal message (or abbreviation thereof) that has meaning to them. Sometimes an entire love story can be read in the inscription of a ring. In 1936 the duke of Windsor (formerly King Edward VIII) gave Wallis Simpson a gargantuan 20-karat emerald engagement ring engraved "We are ours now 27 X 36." The brief inscription was full of meaning for the couple; they often used the word *we* because it was composed of their initials, and the date, October 27, 1936, was the day Mrs. Simpson's divorce was granted, freeing her to marry.

Rings for Men
Wedding rings for men range from the plain, unornamented gold or platinum band, to very ornate designs that include one or more gemstones.

Even with a plain band of precious metal, there are hundreds of variations to consider. The edges might be done in milgraining, which looks like a string of tiny beads. The finish may be shiny, satin, or matte. Actual designs can vary from basketweave to elaborate carving. One popular option is the classic Russian ring, composed of three interconnected bands that together form one ring. Another approach with a gemstone wedding band is to flush-set diamonds into the metal, which gives a smooth, polished look to the ring. Whatever style is chosen, men's rings should be distinctly masculine and understated rather than large and gaudy affairs that look like high school or college rings.

Should the man's ring match his fiancée's? Not necessarily. This is a matter of personal taste, and a man's taste is often quite different from a woman's. Some couples like matching rings; others prefer to select different styles for the man and woman.

Buying Precious Metals

While a few couples opt for wedding rings in sterling silver, the classic choice of metal for wedding rings is either platinum or gold.

Platinum has made a major resurgence in recent years and is considered the precious metal du jour. This lustrous, silvery-white metal was quite fashionable in the early 1900s and many art deco style vintage rings are made with platinum. During the Second World War platinum was categorized as strategic and reserved for military use only. But over the years its popularity has grown, and recently U.S. sales of platinum have skyrocketed.

Platinum is stronger and more durable than gold, which is why platinum settings are often used with gold rings. Platinum will not wear away and become thinner, as can happen with the shank of a gold ring over a period of decades. Scratches in a platinum ring can usually be polished away by a jeweler. Platinum is also hypoallergenic.

This precious metal complements diamonds exquisitely and is often combined with gold accents for a versatile look. Although I personally think platinum and diamonds make the most elegant and timeless combination, even with a ring of yellow gold, platinum or white gold can be used in the setting of a near-colorless diamond to lessen the chance of the stone picking up yellowish glints from the setting.

Four other metals that are members of the platinum family–rhodium, iridium, ruthenium, and palladium–are used either to plate platinum jewelry or in alloys with platinum to increase its hardness. If a ring is 95 percent pure platinum, it can be stamped *PLAT*. If the ring contains a percentage of alloy metal that is larger than 5 percent, the stamp will indicate that. For example, if the piece is marked *IRID-PLAT*, it is 90 percent platinum and 10 percent iridium. Because of their purity, pieces marked *PLAT* are costlier than *IRIDPLAT*.

Platinum is usually somewhat more expensive than 18 karat gold, yet despite its cost platinum has an understated, elegant look.

Gold is the other metal favored for wedding and engagement rings. In its purest form, gold is quite soft and malleable, which is why it can be used in thin sheets as gold leaf. For jewelry gold is alloyed with any of a number of metals, including copper, silver, and nickel, to make it harder and more durable and to give it a desirable color. "White" gold is an alloy of gold, copper, zinc, nickel, and sometimes silver, while "red" or "pink" gold is an alloy of gold, silver, and copper, with the latter giving the rosy color.

Gold is graded according to purity in karats. Pure gold is 24 karat, which is seldom used for jewelry because it is very soft. Alloys of gold show the percentage of gold in fractions of 24. Eighteen-karat gold signifies 18 parts gold out of 24, or 75 percent pure gold. Fourteen-karat gold is 14/24 or 58 percent gold. Real gold jewelry will always be engraved in an inconspicuous place with its karat weight as a mark of quality and purity.

When thinking about the metal for your fiancée's ring, consider what types of jewelry she generally wears. If she loves sterling silver jewelry, you might want to consider a platinum or white gold ring to complement her other pieces. If she likes gold jewelry, she will probably want a gold setting of some sort.

Selecting a Jewel

The diamond is still considered the classic stone for an engagement ring, wedding band, and eternity ring. For many people the purchase of a diamond or gemstone engagement ring is the single largest jewelry purchase they will make. Buying jewelry can be a very complicated affair, and the business is full of unscrupulous sellers. Unless a trusted relative or close friend is a jeweler, you'll want to do some research so that you can ask intelligent questions and get value for your money.

You've heard of the "four C's." These are color, cut, clarity, and karat weight, the four measures on which diamonds are graded. A reputable jeweler will show you written documentation of the diamond's grade in each of these factors.

Color Diamonds vary widely in hue, from colorless to brownish. These colors are graded from D to Z+. Diamonds graded D through F are colorless, extremely rare, and expensive. G through J are near colorless. K through M are faint yellow. N to Z are very light to light yellow, while Z+ is termed fancy yellow and is distinctly golden. It is easiest to distinguish between these grades of color by looking at loose stones under good light in a jeweler's white grading tray. Also, note that colored diamonds have made a resurgence in recent years and that some rare tints can be more expensive than colorless stones.

Cut Cut refers not only to the shape of the diamond but more importantly to the skill with which it has been faceted. A poorly cut diamond may have no more brilliance or fire than a piece of glass. A well-cut diamond is well proportioned, symmetrical, has no flaws in the cut, and is optimally brilliant.

Clarity The clarity of a diamond is graded according to the presence or absence of flaws in the stone. Internal imperfections are termed *inclusions*, while external ones are called *blemishes*. Several systems are used to grade clarity in diamonds, but the best known is that of the Gemological Institute of America (GIA). Your jeweler should disclose the stone's grade and point out any visible flaws using a jeweler's loupe.

Karat Karat weight measures the actual weight, not size, of the stone. Diamonds weighing less than one karat are measured in points, with 100 points to a karat. Therefore a 50-point stone is a half a karat in weight. The cost per karat is not a constant but varies according to the stone's quality, cut, and color. Also, because of their rarity, larger diamonds typically cost more per karat than smaller ones, but not always. A rare colored diamond of two karats can cost far more than a larger colorless diamond.

Diamond Shapes

Diamonds and other gemstones can be cut into a number of shapes and facet styles.

Brilliant The brilliant-cut diamond is the classic cut for a solitaire. Round in shape, the stone has 58 facets, which maximizes its brilliance and fire. Many other fancy cuts, such as the marquise, oval, and pear, are modifications of the brilliant cut.

Emerald This popular cut can range from a square to a long, thin rectangle, although a chunky rectangle is the most common shape. The emerald cut's major feature is a flat plane ("table") at the center of the stone, with facets around it. Because the emerald cut has relatively few facets, it has an almost clear appearance and any flaws in the diamond are more readily seen. Hence the emerald cut is usually done with near-flawless stones.

Marquise or marquis This cut is a variation of the 58-facet brilliant cut, shaped like a boat with two pointed ends.

Oval This cut is another variation on the brilliant, with 58 facets. It can vary in shape from a short, broad oval to long and thin.

Pear The pear-shaped diamond is a variation of the brilliant, having 58 facets. It is actually shaped like a teardrop, not a pear, with one end tapering to a point.

Heart The heart-shaped diamond is a variation of the brilliant. This cut must be well proportioned, with the diameter across the shoulders equal to its length.

Princess The princess, another variation of the brilliant, is usually square shaped and gives the effect of a four-pointed star in the diamond. This cut is primarily used in so-called "channel set" rings, where the diamonds are set edge to edge to look seamless.

Radiant The radiant cut was developed in the 1970s. It combines the sparkle and fire of the brilliant cut with the rectangular shape of the emerald cut. The true radiant cut is an eight-sided square or rectangular diamond with faceted corners.

Trillion or trilliant The trillion cut was created in the late 1970s. In shape, it is an equilateral triangle,

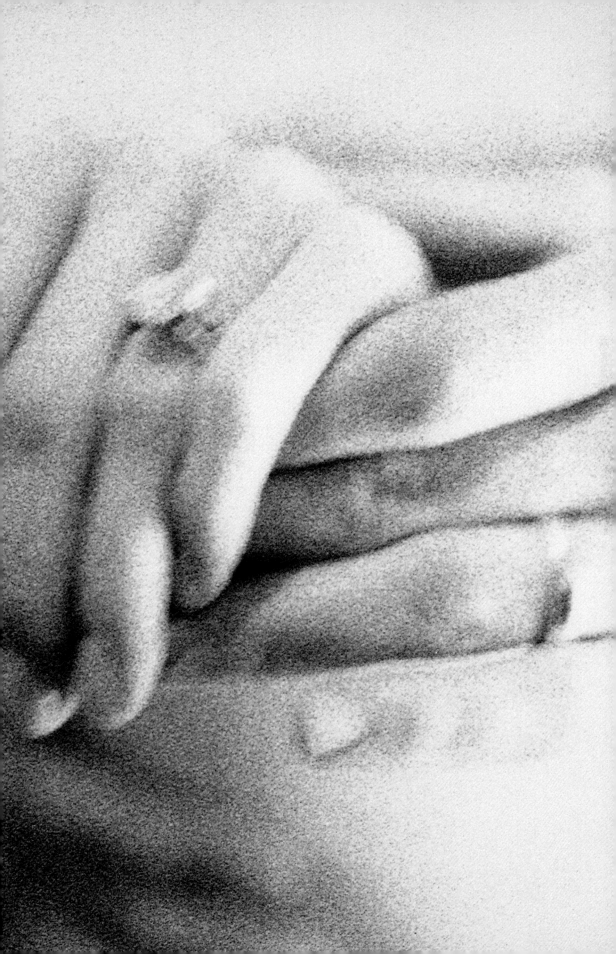

Month	Birthstone
January	Garnet
February	Amethyst
March	Bloodstone, aquamarine
April	Diamond
May	Emerald
June	Pearl, moonstone, or alexandrite
July	Ruby
August	Carnelian, peridot
September	Sapphire
October	Opal, tourmaline
November	Topaz, citrine
December	Turquoise, lapis lazuli, zircon

adapted from the radiant cut. When cut perfectly, trillions have great brilliance and often look larger than their karat weight because they can be quite shallow in depth. A pair of trillions flanking a larger brilliant-cut stone creates a brilliant effect.

Quadrillion This square cut, patented in 1981, has 49 facets and is a sparkly cut. Like the princess, the quadrillion's facets create the effect of a four-pointed star.

The Allure of Colored Gems

Diamonds may be traditional, but many other stones besides diamonds make beautiful engagement rings. Rubies, emeralds, and sapphires are some of the colored stones most often used for engagement rings, but there are other possibilities as well. Perhaps your fiancée would like her birthstone in an engagement ring, or maybe she has a penchant for deep purple amethysts. Precious and semiprecious stones can also be set with diamonds for added sparkle and personal taste.

Keep in mind that with gemstones such as sapphires, rubies, and emeralds, the shade and intensity of color is highly important. A stone that is very dark or light is less valuable than an intensely colored one. Also, choose a stone that is durable. For example, tanzanite is a gorgeous blue-violet gem, but it is relatively soft and fragile, so it is better for a cocktail ring than for one that will be worn daily.

For precious stones as well as diamonds, it is important to obtain third-party documentation from a gemologist.

Trusting a Jeweler

There are several types of jewelers to consider when buying an engagement or wedding ring. The large, well-known international firms such as Tiffany, Cartier, Van Cleef & Arpels, and H. Stern have built tremendous reputations for quality, and their jewelry commands a premium price. Many men don't mind spending a bit more at these established houses to get the reassurance that comes from dealing with such a firm. Another option are the jewelry districts that exist in many cities, which are filled with smaller entrepreneurial firms and where aggressive pricing is customary. If you choose to deal with one of the smaller jewelers, it is critical that you do your homework and understand how to structure the transaction to get your money's worth.

Buying jewelry can be a complicated business, so it is important to find a jeweler who takes the time to explain in detail the attributes and the flaws of a given piece. When evaluating gemstones compare those in your price range with more expensive and less expensive stones, to better understand the features and flaws of each. With any gemstone you should ask to look at an "ideal" cut alongside the stones you are considering. The ideal cut of any gemstone shape is one that is perfectly proportioned and optimally brilliant.

Unless you have a longtime association with a jeweler, ask for recommendations from a trusted friend. I recommend shopping for your engagement ring at no fewer than three establishments. Compare selection, quality, pricing, and service. And certainly, if a jeweler cannot provide documentation for your stone from a gemologist, or refuses to do so, run the other way.

The Bottom Line

There are no hard-and-fast rules about how much to spend on an engagement ring, although the diamond industry would have you believe otherwise. They advise spending two months' salary on the ring. I think that is unrealistic, because people's circumstances and spending habits differ. Some grooms would consider spending two months' salary on a ring to be the height of extravagance. Others might wish to spend even more. It's entirely a personal decision, but keep these points in mind:

• Always work with a reputable jeweler.

• Few people can afford a flawless diamond, but only jewelers can tell the difference between a flawless and a slightly flawed stone. Slightly colored and/or slightly flawed stones can be absolutely gorgeous in the right setting.

• When in doubt, go for brilliance and color.

Chapter 5

Good Intentions

The Engagement

Your engagement, whether it is long or short, is a transition from being a bachelor to thinking of yourself as part of a couple. This is the time to put into place the framework that will forever sustain your commitment to your wife.

Start off on the right road to a long marriage by making sure you and your fiancée have good communication. Communication is key to a successful marriage. Every day it is important for the two of you to spend quality time together. You need to know what's going on in her life, and she needs to understand yours. You may discuss important world issues or tell her the latest joke, but the important thing is to keep the lines of communication open so that you can easily bring up important personal issues and stay focused on your goals as a couple.

You may want to set aside time every day to decompress from business pressures and transition to the evening's activities. I like the cocktail hour and think it is a very civilized ritual that can enhance relationships and foster good communication. It doesn't mean you have to drink alcohol, either. Just ignore the telephone, turn off the television, and pour yourselves a glass of wine, a sparkling water with a spritz of lime, or a tea or coffee. Talk about your day. Tell your wife of your challenges and accomplishments, and catch up with what's going on in her life. You'll find this daily hour to be a wonderful period of time that will help keep your relationship vibrant and each of you focused on the other.

If you are not living with your fiancée, now is the time to truly make her a part of your life. Include her in everything, just as you will after you're married. Introduce her as your wife-to-be to your coworkers, and have her meet all your friends, if she hasn't already.

One of the secrets to a good marriage is for couples to have activities of interest that they like doing together. It might be antiquing, cooking, golfing, or Rollerblading at the beach. Whatever it is, shared interests and passions enrich life and help sustain a long and successful relationship. During your engagement you can start setting the patterns for your life together. The point is that you have to make the effort to keep space in your busy lives for the activities and pursuits that enrich your relationship. When you nurture those shared pleasures, the passion has a greater chance of staying alive.

Details, Details . . .

Your engagement is also the time to get all the legalese and paperwork completed before you are married. Don't procrastinate in taking care of these important details well in advance of your wedding day.

Tasks to handle range from getting any blood tests that may be required, to obtaining the marriage license, changing your wills and life insurance policies to reflect your married status, and finalizing any prenuptial agreements. Some states require birth certificates to obtain a marriage license, so know the requirements in your state to ensure you have the necessary documentation. If your wife is changing her name, or if you are hyphenating your names, this will complicate matters, so it is best to take care of this well in advance. Don't forget to make the appropriate changes to your banking information, insurance policies, and will.

Prenuptial Agreements

If you or your bride has significant assets, children from a previous marriage, or other complicating issues to sort out, it makes sense for each of you to consult with a trusted attorney before you make plans to marry. If a prenuptial agreement is indicated, it should be discussed immediately after the proposal, before plans are made and emotions can get in the way of clear thinking. Introducing the subject of a prenuptial agreement should be done diplomatically, keeping your bride's feelings uppermost in your mind. It may be a difficult subject, but it's much better to settle these issues in advance than to have them cause problems later. Just don't procrastinate; it's unfair to everyone to let discussions of the prenup cast a pall on the preparations for the wedding.

Your Families

When you marry, you're not just marrying the woman; you're marrying her family, for better or worse! If you and your bride have close relationships with your parents, you'll want to maintain those relationships, while nurturing all the new ones that the marriage puts into place. It's important to foster good feelings between your parents and your bride, as well as between her parents and you. Your engagement is an opportunity to start off as a gentleman with your future in-laws and cement the bonds of respect between you. The engagement period is also a time when you make a special effort to allow your parents to get better acquainted with your future in-laws, and vice versa. In the short term there may be wedding-related issues that are difficult to discuss, but in the long run, having both sets of parents getting along can only enhance your wedding celebration.

If both families live in the same community, it should be relatively easy to arrange a get-together as simple as a weekend brunch or a dinner, with both sets of your parents able to enjoy each other's company while breaking bread. In situations where there may have been a divorce or other family schisms, use your best judgment in deciding whether it makes sense to bring everyone together or if a series of separate dinners is a better idea.

Frequently everyone lives in different cities, and arranging a meeting may require you or your fiancée to get on a plane with one set of parents and travel to meet the other. If you have the extra bedrooms, you and your fiancée can host your parents for a weekend. Whatever you decide, the point is that you should make it a priority to foster good relations between your parents and your in-laws. Reach out to your parents and involve them in your lives. If you can't be together, make a point of calling them, with both you and your fiancée on the line. Be sure to remember parental birthdays and anniversaries, as well as Mother's Day and Father's Day, with cards or gifts that come from both you and your fiancée. Both sets of parents will appreciate your thoughtfulness in bringing the families together.

Registering Together as a Couple

Your engagement is a time for you and your bride to plan your home together and register for wedding gifts that you need and that will enhance your lifestyle as a couple. Think carefully about your tastes and style before rushing to the gift registration table and signing up. Talk over your needs and make some overall decisions well in advance of walking into a store. Your bride may be partial to an ornate, gold-rimmed china pattern, but your lifestyle may actually be much more casual. If neither you nor she can boil an egg, it is silly to register for fish poachers and three-hundred-dollar stand mixers. The last thing you should be registering for are items that will gather dust in a cupboard for a decade. Instead, outfit your home with what you need now, the right quantity of china or pottery, glassware, silverware, serving pieces, and cookware that suit your current lifestyle and that can be used on a regular basis. There is always time to purchase that formal collection of china and fine crystal when you are ready. Think about your personal style of entertaining and about the kinds of foods you like to serve. If sushi is your thing, you may want to focus on some well-designed Japanese-style plates and serving pieces from a shop that specializes in Asian tableware, instead of slavishly building up a dozen standard place settings in your pattern. There are no laws that state you must go by the rules of the china store, either. I like to mix and match pieces from different designers and collections to create a more layered, collected look.

The one extravagance I do recommend is registering for a good set of sterling silver (or silver plate) flatware. Good silver is appropriate for any occasion, whether it be informal or formal. With proper care it will last you for the rest of your life. I use my good silver every day and stick it in the dishwasher. It always looks elegant, and the more you use it, the better it looks.

Please remember no one says you *must* register for the traditional items such as china, silver, and crystal. Maybe you're perfectly happy with what you already own. In that case you may elect to register for things you'll use: home electronics, luxurious bed linens, fine wine or champagne, camping equipment, patio furniture, CDs, or a pair of mountain bikes. Your friends will be happy to know their gifts will be truly appreciated and used.

Chapter 6

Planning the Wedding

What Should the Groom Expect?

As I have said before, too many grooms think their only responsibility for the wedding is to show up. But I am a firm believer in the groom being involved in the planning process and incorporating his taste and preferences on an equal basis with those of the bride. You'll be making important decisions jointly throughout your marriage, and your wedding is a great time to start functioning as a team. Remember that your wedding is a turning point in life, not just a big party. It's an opportunity for you and your bride to create a distinctive celebration and make a statement of style to your friends and family as you begin your life together as a couple.

Once you and your fiancée have decided to marry, it's never too early to begin discussions about how you want to ritualize and celebrate your wedding. Before you decide on details such as the date, time, guest list, and location, step back and look at the big picture. I always advocate creating the complete fantasy and finding ways to keep the concept alive while accommodating the budget. Focusing on the big picture first allows you to create a thread of style that can weave its way throughout everything the guests come into contact with, from the invitation to the ceremony, the reception, and the thank-you notes. If you focus on the small details without looking at the big picture, it can be more difficult to get a coherent look and feel for your celebration.

To start the planning process, ask yourself a series of questions about your wedding. What kind of ceremony and reception suits you and your bride? Are you living in the city and prefer "urban chic" cocktail parties, or do you prefer a more casual country feel? Formal or informal? Do you prefer a large gathering of friends and family, or a more intimate setting at a remote location? Will your ceremony be religious, secular, or spiritual? Whatever decisions you make with your fiancée need to suit your style.

Forget about the rules you may have heard that suggest you must serve a sit-down dinner at the reception or the men must wear tuxedos. I encourage couples to look at alternatives that fit their personal taste. Different approaches to consider include a morning civil ceremony downtown, followed by a wedding breakfast with a small group of family members and close friends. Another option can be an informal noontime ceremony with just your best man and maid of honor as witnesses, followed by a casual outdoor picnic in a meadow for the wedding party, family, and friends.

When I begin planning a wedding with a couple, I ask them to answer a series of questions designed to help them define their personal taste, preferences, and style. The answers will relate to all aspects of the wedding celebration, from the food to the music. Couples find it helpful to go over the questions

together and list their answers. Armed with information, it is far easier to make the big decisions on what type and style of wedding celebration is right for both of you.

Questions for You and Your Bride to Consider

1. What are your favorite restaurants? Describe what you like about them–the atmosphere, the type of cuisine, the quality of food, the way the food is served, and perhaps the way the restaurant is decorated. Are there any elements that your favorite restaurants have in common, and if so, what are they and how might you wish to incorporate them into a great wedding reception?

2. What are your favorite foods? Are there specific types of foods–French, Northern Italian, Indian, Japanese, Southwestern barbecue–that you love? What are your least favorite foods? Are there certain dishes from favorite restaurants that you love, such as a grilled vegetable salad, or the way a local bistro prepares duck breast? This information will help you better direct your caterer or banquet manager.

3. What sort of food service do you prefer? Is a formal sit-down dinner your idea of a great party, or do you prefer a buffet, where you can select foods that suit you? Do you enjoy dining casually or formally?

4. What are your favorite drinks? Do you prefer wine, beer, spirits, or soft drinks? Do you have a favorite cocktail? Do you love microbrews?

5. Where do you like to spend your vacation? What appeals to you about the destination, and why? Is it formal or relaxed? Cosmopolitan or rustic? On the beach or in the country?

6. What are your favorite books or stories, and what sort of atmosphere does your favorite book or story create? Are there ways to incorporate elements of this into your wedding celebration?

7. What is your favorite film, and why? Are there scenes from a favorite movie that really appeal to you? Do you remember wedding scenes from films, such as the nuptials in *Four Weddings and a Funeral* or *My Best Friend's Wedding*, that seem to match your style?

8. What is your favorite flower, and if you're unsure, are there flowers you dislike? If you don't know the specific names of flowers, think about what colors and types of flowers appeal to you. Look through books and magazines, and note or clip photos of the ones you like.

9. What are your favorite and least favorite colors? Consider how your favorite colors translate to different types of fabrics that might be used in wedding attire or decor.

10. Does a particular time of day or season of the year inspire you? Do you love sunsets? Do you love the cozy feeling of being indoors after a winter snowfall? Do you love long summer evenings outdoors? Consider how this might affect the timing of your wedding.

11. Do you have a favorite collection that might offer a theme for your wedding? Incorporating a collection of objects that have meaning to you and your bride is an opportunity to personalize your wedding celebration.

12. Do you have a hobby or pursuit that you want to incorporate into your wedding in some way? If a

couple loves to sail, a seaside wedding at a marina, yacht club, or even on a boat might be appropriate. If you love opera, perhaps your celebration should include some of your favorite arias performed by a local opera singer. If you enjoy collecting wine, then fine wine might be a focus of your celebration.

13. What clothing designers are your favorites? What specifically about their designs appeals to you? Is it the lines of the clothing, the use of color, the fabrics? Consider how these can be translated into your own wedding clothing or the overall party decor.

14. Do you see your wedding as a single event, or would you like to have a series of events over several days, such as a weekend-long celebration? Do most of your guests live nearby, or are many traveling to the wedding from out of town?

15. What is your favorite type of music? Make a list of your favorite composers and their works, the artists and their songs. Be sure to make a short list of the music you definitely do *not* want to hear at your wedding as well!

18. What are your favorite photographic styles? Do you like black and white, color, or sepia? Do you like a photojournalistic, documentary, or traditional portrait approach? Remember that you can expect to look at your wedding pictures for decades to come, so be sure to determine the approach and style that suits you and your bride.

19. When you can do absolutely anything, or nothing at all, how do you spend the day? Would you love to spend an afternoon shooting the breeze with friends over a couple of beers, or would you prefer a great hike in the mountains? How could you translate your preferences to your wedding day?

20. Do you have a visual image of your wedding? Whether the answer is yes or no, another good exercise is to look through as many magazines as possible and tear out pictures of things you and your fiancée like and dislike. The more visual images you have when you meet with your vendors, the easier it will be to paint a clear picture of your personalities and taste.

Once you have the answers to these questions written down, you can begin to see what style of wedding is right for you. The important thing to remember is to keep a consistent thread of style that weaves through all the elements of the wedding, from the invitations, the ceremony, the flowers, the food, the drinks, and the music, to the thank-you notes for wedding presents.

Early in your engagement you should decide with your bride and both families whether to use the services of a wedding consultant or party planner. The decision depends on several factors: the scale of your wedding, how much time all of you have to devote to the design and planning process, and how capable you feel of managing the many small details involved. A talented, capable, and organized wedding planner can mean a lot less stress on you, your bride, and your families.

A referral from a trusted friend or associate whose taste you admire is the best way to find a good wedding planner. Other resources include the food and beverage managers of top hotels or leading florists and caterers who often work on weddings. Be sure to interview several candidates so that you can compare services and pricing. Look for someone you have rapport with and who is receptive to your input. If you have trouble getting the person on the phone during initial discussions, beware–it won't get any easier! Finally, obtain confirmation that the wedding consultant with whom you plan your arrangements will manage your event personally on site and not just send an associate.

Whatever style of wedding you and your fiancée prefer, as the groom you need to decide early on how involved you want to be in the planning process, and make sure your bride understands and is supportive of your role. Each of you has strengths and talents that you bring to the tasks ahead. Perhaps you want to make all the important decisions about your wedding together, as a couple. Or maybe you want to leave most of the planning and decision making to your bride, with certain areas, such as wines and spirits, music and cigars, to be left up to you. In many instances couples prefer to divide the project, so that you handle certain areas and your fiancée takes care of others. If you're a computer whiz, maybe you could take on the development and maintenance of the guest and response list. If you have excellent organizational skills, you could create a schedule for the ceremony and reception and a to-do list with all the tasks that must be accomplished.

Don't be locked into a typical groom role if your talents lie elsewhere. Perhaps you have little interest in music but are a connoisseur of food and wine. Maybe you have a talent for aesthetics and decor and want to work with the florist on the visual concept for the reception. Whatever seems right for you, the important thing is that you decide with your fiancée what your separate and joint roles will be, and are supportive of each other's efforts.

Keep in mind that if you divide wedding-related responsibilities with your bride, the vendors with whom you are working need to have one individual as their contact and decision maker. Be sure that vendors know which of you they are to deal with on issues requiring input or decisions.

Here are some areas of responsibility for you to consider assuming:

• The groom who loves fine dining may decide to work directly with the caterer or hotel on the menu. As a word of caution, don't get carried away–remember that a complicated menu can cause the budget to skyrocket and may be difficult for the chef to execute properly.

• If you are interested in wine, offer to select and secure the wines for the celebration. Once you have the menu, you may select the wine yourself from the list the hotel or caterer provides, or you may fax your menu to the best wine retailer in town for him or her to help you pick the wines. Of course, if you ask a retailer to select the wines on your behalf, you would be expected to purchase the wines from that retailer. Avoid wasting anyone's time, your own included.

• If your interest in wine extends to fine spirits, perhaps you also want to work with your hotel or caterer to approve the brands of spirits offered, and maybe even choose one or two specialty cocktails to be tray-passed during the reception. Guests love to be offered an interesting cocktail that they might not have otherwise chosen. A great cocktail gets the party off to a quick and happy start. Some of my favorites include flavored vodka martinis, cosmopolitans, mint juleps, and even gimlets.

• Transportation of the wedding party can be a complicated logistical challenge. Depending on your budget, the solution may range from asking wedding guests with spacious cars to drive groups of guests, to renting vans or limousines and hiring drivers. If you have good organizational abilities, you can take on the transportation logistics to ensure that everyone gets where they need to be in style. Give special thought to the transportation you arrange for yourself and the bride as you leave the wedding reception. A horse-drawn carriage may be a great idea if you are to be married in the country (or in a city such as New York that offers such transportation), or a friend might loan a vintage Mercedes road-ster or a Rolls-Royce convertible so that the two of you can make a dramatic exit in front of the guests.

• Are you the one in the marriage with the thousand-CD collection? Perhaps you want to take on the task of working with the band or other musicians. You should confirm well in advance issues such as when the band must arrive, what they will wear, how many breaks they will take, how long the breaks are, and when the breaks will occur. Also, be sure to provide the bandleader with a list of songs you'd like to hear throughout the event, and songs you definitely don't want played. Don't forget to tell the bandleader which song should be played for your first dance. You could also put together a compilation tape to be played when the band is on break, as there should be some music playing at all times.

• For the cigar-loving groom, there is perhaps no sweeter smoke than the one shared with friends at his wedding reception. Providing a few boxes of fine cigars is another responsibility you might want to assume, perhaps in consultation with your father or the bride's father if they also enjoy a good smoke. One elegant way to do the cigar presentation is to have a waiter roll a cart through the reception area, offering guests cigars and the use of a cutter and cigar matches. Just one word of advice: Don't let a box of expensive cigars circulate unattended. You have no idea how greedily otherwise well-mannered men can behave when faced with a box of free Cohibas.

Consensus and Compromise

Despite everyone's best intentions, couples planning their wedding often find themselves in conflict with their parents or others who wish to be involved in the planning process. Take it from me: *Everyone* will have something to say about your party. Others may mean well, but this is your day, and every bride and groom should have the wedding that is right for them. It is important to set ground rules early on, so that you don't get steamrollered into agreeing with wedding elements that don't suit you. It is equally important, however, to maintain an atmosphere of give-and-take when it comes to family diplo-macy. Compromise is often the best approach when there's an issue that is causing a major conflict.

When you think about it, planning your wedding with your fiancée and both families is an ideal opportunity to step up to the plate and use your talents. After all, a typical wedding is a lot like a complicated, expensive business deal. It involves research, interviewing vendors, planning, scheduling, negotiation, and a lot of hand-holding for the interested parties. There's a valuable role for a groom who can act as mediator and counselor, offering input while remaining aware of everyone's priorities and interests. You can also practice your skills at negotiation. Trust me when I inform you that there has never been a more delicate bargaining session than when a bride is intent on one specific aspect of her wedding ceremony, while her mother, and perhaps your parents, have different ideas. By helping everyone to reach consensus without tears or bloodshed, you can come out of the bargaining session looking like the ideal husband and son-in-law.

A wedding would hardly be a wedding if it didn't evoke some family conflict. Whenever you assemble an extended family, tensions often ensue. Your job is to make sure, as much as possible, that people don't lose sight of the fact that this is a joyous occasion uniting two people in love. If family members are using your wedding as an opportunity to exacerbate family tensions, tactfully put a stop to it. The situation may require you to be explicit; for example, saying, "Mother, I understand that you don't want Dad's new wife in the wedding photos, but she is part of our family now, and it wouldn't be right to exclude her. I'll make sure you aren't seated anywhere near her and Dad during the reception. And remember to save your first dance for me, okay?"

When it comes to making difficult wedding-related decisions, your job is to stand behind your fiancée and form a united front—unless, of course, you disagree with her, in which case you should discuss the situation with her privately and come to an agreement. Remember, you're making a lifetime commitment to your fiancée, for better or worse. She'll need a lot of coddling and support as the days and weeks tick off before the wedding, so be sure you're there for her.

A Calendar and Checklist

Six to Twelve Months Before the Wedding

Make decisions about the style of wedding you want.

Set a tentative date and time for the wedding, pending confirmation that the location you want is available.

Determine the budget.

Research locations, and book the space.

Retain the officiant for the ceremony.

Begin developing the guest list.

Research wedding vendors, such as florist, caterer, photographer, and band.

Ask your best man, groomsmen, and ushers (if you have them) to serve, and inform them of all pertinent dates.

Interview photographers and videographers.

Work with your fiancée in selecting your registry items.

Three to Six Months Before the Wedding

If you will be renting formalwear, research shops in your area and place your order. Obtain measurement cards for out-of-town groomsmen, father of the bride, and be sure they are filled out and returned to the store.

If you are buying wedding attire, shop for a suit or formalwear. Allow two to three months for custom tailoring.

Check the requirements for blood tests, physical exams, and the marriage license in the state where you will be married.

Shop for wedding rings, allowing time to have them engraved if desired.

Begin planning the honeymoon. Popular destinations during the high season may

need to be booked three to six months in advance (or more).

Finalize the guest list.

Have invitations (and personal stationery, if desired) designed and printed.

Make final selection of wedding vendors, and sign contracts.

Plan the type of rehearsal dinner you will have, and book the space.

Reserve blocks of rooms, if necessary, for out-of-town wedding guests.

Book wedding-night accommodations, if they are different from honeymoon accommodations.

Hire wedding-related transportation (vans, limousines), if necessary.

Discuss and finalize best man's duties.

Designate head usher, if necessary, and brief him on duties.

Mail measurement cards to wedding-party members.

Make honeymoon air travel, ground transportation, and hotel arrangements.

Two to Three Months Before the Wedding

Finalize details with wedding vendors.

Finalize details of ceremony with officiant.

Finalize rehearsal dinner details.

Book massage professional for morning of wedding day.

Book wedding-related grooming professionals (facialist, manicurist), as needed.

Plan and schedule bachelor party or weekend.

Have a blood test and physical exam.

Purchase wedding-party gifts.

Four to Six Weeks Before the Wedding

Mail wedding and rehearsal dinner invitations.

Begin writing thank-you notes with bride for wedding presents.

Compose, design, and print ceremony program, if necessary.

Select boutonnieres for yourself and your groomsmen.

Schedule formalwear fittings, and ensure that all out-of-town measurements have been received.

Arrange with best man to invite friends to bachelor party.

Assist fiancée in confirming all wedding vendor contracts and deposits.

Make changes to banking information, insurance policies, wills, and other legal documents.

Two Weeks Before the Wedding

Double-check and reconfirm all wedding-related arrangements.

Call guests who failed to respond to wedding invitation to find out if they are attending.

Get haircut, facial, and teeth cleaning.

Obtain marriage license with fiancée.

Pick up wedding rings from jeweler.

Double-check and confirm all honeymoon travel arrangements.

During the Week Before the Wedding

Pick up men's wedding attire, and have final fittings.

Give final guest count to caterer or hotel.

Pack for honeymoon and reconfirm arrangements.

Assemble all elements of your wedding attire.

Attend the bachelor party.

The day before the wedding, have a professional manicure.

Prepare wedding gratuities and checks for balances due to vendors.

Attend the rehearsal dinner, and get to bed early!

The Wedding Day

Have a relaxing massage.

Dress with help of best man.

Have wedding gift and note delivered to bride.

Pin on boutonniere.

Join best man and ushers at ceremony site forty-five minutes before ceremony.

Focus on your bride's enjoyment while having a great time yourself!

Chapter 7

Dollars and Sense

Everyone who has a wedding, no matter how much they intend to spend, must deal with the vexing issue of the budget. Trust me: I have worked on weddings that cost tremendous sums of money, and even they had budgets within which we had to work. Whether the budget for your wedding is large or small, your objective is to squeeze the most value out of the dollars you have to spend. The amount of money you have to spend will have an impact on virtually every aspect of the event, from where it is held, to the number of guests that will be invited, to the food and beverages that will be served, so it is absolutely critical that you pay attention to the budget.

There isn't any getting around the fact that weddings are expensive. If you have never been exposed to the cost of hosting a special event in a hotel, restaurant, or club, the price tag of a typical wedding reception may shock you. And remember that the wedding budget must cover more than just the reception food and beverage costs. Invitations, fees for the officiant and ceremony site, wedding attire, transportation, flowers, photography, gifts for the attendants, gratuities, and the honeymoon retreat all carry a price tag. Considered on their own, each item may seem affordable, but when you add everything up, the total can make even the wealthiest people feel faint.

So before you book the limos or place the order for the expensive cigars and fine vintage champagne, it's important to determine a ballpark figure for what you can spend. If you and/or your bride are paying for your own wedding, setting the budget should be a relatively straightforward process. Often, however, the bride's or groom's family is involved in paying for parts of the wedding. In such a case the bride and groom should sit down with their parents and have a frank discussion about the wedding budget.

There's no industry standard cost for a wedding. Those hosting the wedding need to decide what is appropriate for their budget given the type of event that is desired and the financial resources of the parties involved. Common sense should prevail when looking at the numbers. It is foolhardy for a young couple just beginning their careers to go into debt to pay for their wedding, just as it is insensitive for an older bride with a well-paying job to expect her parents, who live on a modest fixed income, to foot the bill for a lavish reception. As a couple, you have to take a close, hard look at your own financial circumstances and those of the others who are contributing, and decide on a sensible budget that works for everyone.

In the past it was a given fact that the bride's parents paid for the wedding and the groom's family hosted the rehearsal dinner. While that was the traditional manner in which wedding expenses were divided, it is no longer the rule but rather the exception. Today it is common for the bride's and the groom's families to share wedding-related expenses. Another common situation occurs when the bride's parents are divorced and a mother and father are each contributing to the wedding separately. In such a situation the bride and groom must use all their relationship skills, tact, and diplomacy to ensure that costs are distributed fairly and the wedding doesn't become a bone of contention among everyone involved.

One popular way to allocate funds for a wedding is for the parents to contribute a set amount. If the bride and groom want to spend more than what is being given to them, they can make up the difference themselves. This approach also gives the couple the option of reserving some of the money for other major expenses, such as the honeymoon or even a down payment on a home.

If the budget for your wedding is very limited, you and your fiancée need to be sensitive to the financial constraints. In such a case perhaps a more intimate ceremony and reception at one of your parents' homes is more appropriate than a large event at a hotel or club. There are no rules that say you must invite guests for dinner and dancing. Perhaps a wedding breakfast, luncheon, or even afternoon tea, which costs much less than dinner, would be a lovely way to celebrate your marriage—and just as chic.

Deciding who should pay for what is another sensitive issue. Don't let old-fashioned ideas of traditional roles shape your expectations. Everyone's circumstances are different, and you and your fiancée are probably the best judges of what is appropriate in your situation. In general I feel that those who have the greatest resources should shoulder a larger portion of the expenses, particularly if there are widely divergent financial circumstances involved. If your fiancée's parents are financially capable, they might generously offer to pay for the entire wedding and even related expenses such as the rehearsal dinner and travel expenses for the wedding party. If you, the groom, are more financially secure while your parents are not, it is appropriate that you step up to the plate and offer to handle a major portion of the wedding expenses.

It often happens that the parents may have ample financial resources but choose to limit their contribution toward the wedding for any number of reasons. It is then up to you and your bride to either make up the difference on your own or to scale back your celebration to fit your budget constraints. As a true gentleman, you should graciously accept what is offered and adjust your plans accordingly.

Traditional Expenses for the Groom
Certain wedding-related expenses are traditionally the groom's responsibility, or the responsibility of the groom's family. Today many grooms still pay for some or all of these expenses, but it is no longer an automatic assumption that these are the groom's costs. I have listed those expenses that are traditionally considered the groom's so that you are aware of what others may expect.

Engagement ring

Wedding rings

Gifts for your best man and ushers

Marriage license

Officiant's fee

Your wedding attire

Wedding present for the bride

Bridal bouquet, corsages for both mothers and other close female relatives, and boutonnieres for the men in the wedding party

Wedding transportation, e.g. limousines, shuttle buses, Town Cars

Gratuities

Honeymoon

Once you have a budget for the wedding, the next challenge is to stay within its limits. Be straightforward in talking about your budget with your wedding consultant and your vendors. Let them know how much you have to spend and that you need detailed, itemized estimates in order to evaluate everything properly. If an estimate seems unusually high, inquire how it was developed and look at the details. Ask the consultant or vendor to suggest ways the estimate can be reduced. There's room in every budget to make reductions if needed. Once you have selected a vendor, insist on a written contract with all the commitments and costs spelled out. Be sure that the contract covers all aspects of the services you expect–arrival times, what the service people will be wearing, when overtime expenses start to accrue, and so on. You want everything spelled out in detail beforehand to avoid any later confusion. As with all contracts, read the fine print very carefully to avoid hidden costs and other surprises.

When Price Is Not an Issue

A few words of advice: If your fiancée tells you the price of her wedding dress, don't let your jaw drop and gasp, "What?" This applies particularly if you have seen her in the dress. Just nod thoughtfully, and if you've seen the dress, "That certainly was money well spent, darling. It looks wonderful on you." Or if you haven't seen the dress, say, "That sounds about right." Your fiancée wants to know that you support her in this important and emotionally charged decision.

If vendors have been suggested by the hotel, club, or other facility where you will be holding the ceremony or reception, always ask if the vendor is paying a commission to the person who recommended them. Frequently banquet managers, wedding consultants, and others within the industry receive commissions from favored vendors. Not only may this inflate the cost to you as the client, but the recommendation may be based on the commission paid and not on the vendor's suitability to your event.

If you are adept at using a computerized spreadsheet, you can track estimates and keep a constant running total of the budgeted items as they come in. A good system is a great help not only for keeping track of costs but for making sure nothing is overlooked in the planning process. Finally, build in a contingency fund, usually 10 to 15 percent of your budget, since there will always be unanticipated costs. Your contingency fund will allow you to handle unexpected expenses without creating a major fiscal crisis. It's always best to budget on the high side and be happily surprised when your expenses are lower than originally anticipated.

Chapter 8

Defining the Wedding Party

Choosing a Best Man

I suspect that everyone who has served as the best man in a wedding, and who has picked up a typical wedding book a few days before his duties are to begin, felt shocked at what he was expected to handle! In fact, traditionally the duties of the best man included a daunting laundry list of obligations. Did you know, according to the 1957 edition of *The Amy Vanderbilt Complete Book of Etiquette*, "the best man is adviser, messenger, valet, secretary, and general factotum to the groom"? This book's list of the best man's duties spans an entire page and includes waking up the groom on the day of the wedding and packing the wedded couple's car trunk with their luggage for the honeymoon. I must admit that in all the years I have planned weddings, I have never come across a best man who fulfilled even 10 percent of Ms. Vanderbilt's traditionally mandated duties!

Today it is rare for the best man to do more than keep the bride's wedding ring in his coat pocket and make the first toast to the bride and groom. Most best men seem to think their duties are strictly ceremonial. While today's attitude toward the role of the best man is more relaxed, I think it's a very good idea to select an individual who will assume some responsibility in the wedding. A capable best man can relieve you, the groom, of many wedding-related details, helping to keep you relaxed as the day approaches. Here are some ideas to consider:

1. If your best man has good taste in clothing, it can be helpful to have him accompany you to select your wedding attire.

2. The best man can be designated to pick out gifts from the groom to the ushers. These gifts are generally given to the ushers at the rehearsal dinner.

3. Since the bachelor party is often the responsibility of the best man, it is important that the person you select as best man will make appropriate choices in theme and entertainment for your bachelor party.

4. The best man can help with your personal logistics and transportation to and from the wedding, making sure you get where you are supposed to be, and that your luggage and that of your bride is safely stowed as necessary.

5. On the day of your wedding, the best man should hold the bride's wedding ring, handing it to you at the appropriate point in the ceremony. If you have a ring bearer, the best man is responsible for the ring until it is given to the ring bearer.

6. The best man is usually entrusted to handle payment to the officiant. This may be done before or after the ceremony. One of the advantages of having the best man handle this detail is that it keeps your rela-

Coaxing the Ring Bearer

I learned a wonderful trick that comes in handy if you have a young ring bearer who experiences a sudden crisis and feels too shy to walk down the aisle. Try putting some wrapped candy in your pocket before the ceremony. Then have the ring bearer's mother tell him that you have a special sweet treat for him in your pocket. You will be amazed at how that will restore the confidence and quicken the step of a young child. He'll stride right up to you like a trouper, with hand out ready for his reward.

tionship with the officiant on a more personal level.

7. The first toast is typically the responsibility of the father of the bride to welcome the guests, followed by the best man's toast to the bride and groom.

8. If formalwear has been rented, the best man can be in charge of collecting the apparel from the groom and ushers after the wedding and returning it to the formalwear shop promptly.

If you decide to have your best man assume some or all of these responsibilities, the most important thing is that you and he know for certain who is handling what. You want to avoid the situation where each of you thought the other was responsible for a task that ends up not happening.

Typically the best man is the groom's brother, cousin, or close friend, although the groom's father is often designated best man. Whomever you select, be sure that the person has the time and ability to help with the responsibilities you wish him to handle. Avoid selecting a best man who is chronically late, painfully shy, or generally unreliable. Likewise, don't select someone who has a problem with alcohol, as–unfortunately–weddings are often occasions for overindulgence. There are few things worse than a best man making a toast that is slurred and incomprehensible and drags on past the two minutes allotted.

Great Gift Ideas for the Best Man and Groomsman

Typically, the groom selects a gift for his best man and groomsmen as a thank-you for their support.

Here are several options for traditional and nontraditional gifts.

Traditional

- Monogrammed silver hip flask filled with a favorite alcoholic beverage, such as single-malt scotch or bourbon
- Silver cigar case, monogrammed and dated
- Cuff links or studs for wedding attire
- Monogrammed business card holder
- Monogrammed penknife

- Monogrammed and dated money clip
- Watch engraved with wedding date

Nontraditional

- Tickets or a season pass to sporting events

- A bottle of fine wine or a box of cigars
- Theater or opera tickets—two per person
- Tickets to a music concert
- Gift certificate for a massage at a spa, health club, or resort hotel
- Gift certificate to a favorite restaurant
- The latest electronic organizer or gizmo

The Groomsmen

The groomsmen or ushers are typically responsible for seating guests at the ceremony site, whether it be a church, synagogue, or secular location. Generally, the rule of thumb is one usher for every fifty guests; however, there should be as many ushers as bridesmaids, so don't worry if your usher-to-guest ratio isn't exact. The groom's brothers, cousins, other relatives, or good friends may serve as ushers. The eldest or most responsible male should be head usher, whose responsibility is to make sure all the other ushers show up appropriately attired, on time, and fully cognizant of the duties they are to perform.

The ushers should arrive at the ceremony site forty-five minutes to an hour before the ceremony is to begin. When guests begin to arrive, the ushers should ask if they wish to be seated on the bride's side or the groom's side, and then escort the guests to their seats. The ushers are expected to give their arm to unescorted ladies and to converse pleasantly with guests while they are walking down the aisle. The ushers should also make sure that the front rows remain reserved for immediate family, if so desired.

The important thing to remember about your wedding party is that you should delegate responsibility for the ushers to the head usher or best man. Let either of them make sure that everyone else knows what time they are to arrive and where they are supposed to stand. You shouldn't have to worry about your ushers on your wedding day.

Chapter 9

Whom to Invite

One of the most important issues to decide when planning your wedding is the guest list: whom to invite to witness your vows and share in your celebration. It is an honor to be invited, and your guest list should be composed of the people nearest and dearest to you and your bride. That may turn out to be four hundred people, or it may be twenty. Believe it or not, it is the unusual wedding where the bride and groom have the final say on the guest list. Actually it's inaccurate to talk about "the guest list," because there usually are at least three or four wedding guest lists and sometimes more. Lists come from the bride and groom, their parents, and perhaps other close relatives.

The first step in developing your wedding guest list is for you to sit down with your bride and make up your own list. If your bride's parents are hosting the wedding, or even if not, they will want to invite their own guests as well. Your parents will also have a group of friends and relatives, who may have been left off your list, to invite. You can quickly see how the guest list can swell to proportions unanticipated when the original wedding budget was developed.

Figuring out who should be invited from everyone's lists can become a juggling act as you try to balance everyone's suggestions. Remember that for your parents and your future in-laws, the wedding is a major event that they wish to share with their friends, even if some of them are not close to you or the bride. As you work on the lists, keep in mind the following:

• Generally wedding guest lists are balanced with approximately equal numbers of guests from the bride's side and the groom's. But it often occurs that one side of the family has a much larger guest list, such as if the wedding is being held in the bride's hometown and the groom's family lives out of town.

• If the bride's family is paying for the wedding, and the groom's family wishes to invite more guests than the original estimate included, the groom's family may offer to pay a proportional share of the reception expenses.

• It is socially appropriate to invite an unmarried, unattached person without adding "and guest" to the invitation. It is not appropriate to invite one half of a married couple, one half of a couple living together, or one half of an engaged couple. If a single person is on the guest list and you know he or she is seeing someone seriously, it is thoughtful to invite both.

• If you do not want children at the wedding or reception, do not invite them. A wedding invitation requests only the presence of the people whose names actually appear on the envelope. If guests ask if they can bring their kids, make a diplomatic answer, such as "We regret that we are only inviting a specific number of guests and we are at the limit." Then be sure you don't allow any exceptions; your

The Guest List: Spelling Counts!

You would be surprised at the condition of the guest lists I have seen and how many problems can arise because of a sloppily written or carelessly compiled list. The better prepared you are with your list, the more you will minimize mistakes, which can be costly. It is best to develop the guest list on a personal computer, making sure from the beginning that all spellings, addresses, and phone numbers are correct. With a good database program, you can code the names so that it will be easy to print various subsets of the list, such as a list of those attending the rehearsal dinner, those coming from out of town, or those needing transportation. Don't forget titles such as *Dr., The Honorable,* or *Mr. and Mrs.* An accurate guest list can also be easily handed over to a calligrapher, if you are using one, to write place cards for assigned seating at the reception.

friends who were turned down will be upset to see other people's children at the wedding (except for any children who are actually in the wedding party).

• Think carefully about sending wedding invitations to people who you know have no intention of attending. This can look like a solicitation for wedding gifts. If there are people you would like to inform about the wedding but who you know will not attend, it is more appropriate to send them a wedding announcement. Announcements are usually mailed the day after the wedding. Of course, if there are people who you know will not or cannot attend but might feel slighted if they did not receive an invitation, then by all means send one.

Often it turns out that there are more people who should be invited to your wedding than the budget can accommodate. Your options are either to prioritize the list and remove guests, or to scale back on your plans for the reception. Cutting back on your list is never easy, and you should never be in a position of having to cut close friends from your guest list. If you find yourself having to do that, perhaps your design concept for the wedding reception may be too grand.

I always think it's a better idea to have a party one can afford than to overextend your financial resources. To scale back, consider an alternative approach, such as cocktail party, a clambake on the beach, a Sunday morning brunch, or an outdoor luncheon. If your finances are limited, it is perfectly proper to plan your wedding to occur between meals and feature a delicious sparkling wine punch and wedding cake at your reception.

Nikki and Cosmo

May 23, 1998

...on and Mrs. Robert Jubelirer ~ 21
...d Mrs. Esiri Karu ~ 20
...Mrs. Robert Kaufman ~ 30
...dia Kaup ~ 2
...ney Kaup ~ 13
...s. Rex Kaup ~ 26
...s. David Knapp ~ 37
... Koch ~ 13
...ph Guzza ~ 13
...Kornhaber ~ 4
...ri Stern ~ 4
...rancis Kudrick ~ 31
...n Kudrick ~ 31
...rard Kanni ~ 30
...ng ~ 12

Ms. ...
and M...
Mr. La...
Mr. Jas...
Mr. and M...
Dr. and M...
Mr. and Mr...
Mr. and Mr...
Mr. Michael...
and Andrea...

Chapter 10

What to Wear

What's your style? Preppie, hip, jock, intellectual, conservative, bohemian, fashion slave–whatever your style of clothing, your wedding attire should reflect it. Your clothing should flatter your physique and suit your skin and hair coloring. This is one time when you want to look confident and completely at ease. You can't do that if you're decked out in some costume that just isn't you.

There has long been an unwritten rule that the tuxedo is the groom's uniform. It just isn't so. What a groom wears at his wedding is not only dependent on his personal style but on the time of day, level of formality, and type of event. I get tired of seeing all the men at weddings dressed like penguins. I've even run across weddings where the couple was obviously on a budget and had been forced to skimp on such basics as the buffet, but they were still wearing the fanciest of formal attire. How much more gracious it would have been to cut back on the ball gowns and the tuxedo rentals and spend the money on food and beverages for the guests!

I'm going to make a revolutionary suggestion. Formalwear should be reserved for formal weddings. Furthermore, tuxedos are evening attire; they should never be worn before six P.M. (The only occasions for which black tie can correctly be worn in the afternoon are broadcast events, such as the Academy Awards, when the show begins in Los Angeles in late afternoon to accommodate the three-hour time difference on the East Coast, where it's broadcast live during prime time.)

When you're considering what to wear at your wedding, think first about the time of day, level of formality, and location. A midsummer, midafternoon wedding outdoors under a tent might call for a linen suit for the groom, perhaps in a cream, beige, or pale olive shade. A navy blue blazer paired with a crisp white shirt, colorful tie, and khaki trousers is another great look that works for afternoons or casual summer affairs.

An intimate ceremony and reception at home, scheduled for four P.M. on an autumn afternoon, is the occasion for a dark suit, perhaps enlivened with a new tie and, of course, your boutonniere. However, a church wedding followed by a dinner reception for two hundred at a hotel ballroom calls for a more formal approach such as a tuxedo or, for a very formal wedding, white tie and tails.

If you do plan a formal daytime wedding, the appropriate attire for you and your ushers is the so-called morning coat, a cutaway coat with tails, gray striped trousers, and a waistcoat, worn with a starched shirt and dress ascot or standard tie. At all but the most formal of daytime weddings, the groom and his groomsmen appear much more distinguished in well-tailored suits or in jacket and tie.

The groom also must make sure that his attire complements that of his bride. If your bride has decided on a chic, understated designer gown, your suit or dinner jacket should also be of a contemporary cut and fabric. Likewise, if she has selected a dress with a vintage look, your wedding attire might reflect hers by including a vest in a rich, antique-looking brocade. If she's chosen to wear a color other than white, you can work within the same color family in your suit, shirt, or tie. Obtain a sample of the bride's dress color, and use it to select appropriate colors for your attire. For example, if she is wearing a champagne satin gown, you could pick up that color in a silk tie. Or if you really want to push the envelope, you could have a tieless shirt made out of the same fabric as her gown.

Finally, the groom should consider the financial situation of his groomsmen and whether, in opting for tuxedos, he is asking them to assume an expense that they can ill afford. It's all very well and good to decide that the wedding party will wear white tie and tails, but if that means one of your groomsmen is going to be embarrassed because he can't afford to lay out the rental cost, it's probably not the most thoughtful approach–unless, of course, you are covering the expenses associated with your groomsmen's attire.

The Tux

If you are having a formal wedding, there are myriad options in formalwear. Today's designers are showing tuxedos in an incredible variety of styles and cuts. You may see everything from one-button to five-button dinner jackets, shawl or notched collars, shown in both single- and double-breasted styles. While tuxedos are available in a range of fabrics, I have found that wool crepe or silk-wool blends work best. They are light enough for comfort and drape beautifully. Black is the most classic color, but midnight blue and dark gray can work well for many occasions.

In recent years many formalwear designers have introduced innovations to the tuxedo to update the classic ensemble. The plain black silk-satin cravat has made a reappearance and lends an Edwardian look to formalwear. Many grooms opt to go tieless, wearing instead a formal shirt with a turn-down collar and a decorative button. A formal shirt with a mandarin collar, again worn without a tie, is another option. Donning an antique fabric vest instead of a tie is another way to go.

It is also a nice touch to match the colors of the men's accessories to the wedding colors themselves. But the hues have to be appropriate for the men's attire. Don't let anyone talk you into having all the groomsmen wear matching pink vests, cummerbunds, and bow ties because the bridesmaids are wearing pink! Soft colors such as pink tend to be best on women, while dark shades of blue, green, or gray look better on men.

There are even novel approaches to tuxedo trousers. Jonathan Meizler and Germàn Valdivia, who own the Los Angeles clothing store JonValdì and who have dressed many of the grooms at the weddings on which I work, often design tuxedo pants cut just like slim jeans, which are very flattering and contemporary when worn with a tuxedo jacket cut like a suit coat and a shirt that requires no tie.

At the wedding the closely fitted pants look as polished as the traditional style. After the event the trousers can be worn with a great sweater or contrasting jacket.

Perhaps you already own a tuxedo that you haven't worn in a couple of years. Now is the time to get it out of the closet and scrutinize its style. Does it still fit? If not, take it to a good tailor to see if it can be adjusted. It may also be possible to have your old tuxedo restyled, changing the lapels or making other adjustments to bring it up to date. Another approach is simply to update your accessories. Add a silk vest, a new formal shirt, new cuff links and studs, or even a new bow tie. It's amazing how the right accessory can change the entire look.

If you don't own a workable black-tie ensemble and you are having a formal wedding, you must decide between renting or buying. The main consideration is how often you expect to attend future black-tie occasions. If the answer is "frequently," a tuxedo in a classic style is an excellent investment. Rented tuxedos seldom fit as well as your own, and the headache of renting one every few months can be burdensome.

If you want to wear a tuxedo but are convinced that you will never again have the occasion to sport one, renting is not your only option. Consider creating the look of formalwear with an elegant single-breasted black suit. Prada and Gucci are showing their formal tuxedos being worn with black button-down shirts and a standard black tie. The look is elegant and understated. If it's a little too progressive for your taste, wear your own black suit with a formal white shirt and black silk-satin vest with a high gorge (neckline). The vest will transform your black suit into a dinner jacket. And for even more of a tuxedo look, have your tailor add buttons covered with black silk-satin to your suit. They can be replaced with conventional buttons after the wedding. The look is both polished and formal, and is accomplished without throwing your money away on a tuxedo that you feel certain you will wear only once. And if you don't own a black suit, now is the time to make the investment. A good black suit is a wardrobe staple.

If you are renting, you should select your formalwear and all accessories two to three months before your wedding, reserving time for final fittings about forty-eight hours before the apparel is to be picked up. If your groomsmen will also need to rent formalwear, it is desirable to place the entire order with one establishment so that you can obtain the same style and fabric and possibly arrange for a discount. The shop will provide you with measurement cards that can be faxed or mailed to out-of-town groomsmen and others in the wedding party. Be sure everyone allocates time for a final fitting before the wedding. With a large order it is sometimes possible to negotiate "extras" such as a free rental for the father of the groom or bride. After the wedding the best man is usually entrusted with the task of returning the groom's and other men's apparel to the store promptly.

One of the problems with renting tuxedos is that you can end up with a "rented" look. But there are some creative ways that this can be avoided. Perhaps, as the groom, you might buy new formal dress

Measurements Needed for Groom/Groomsmen

Coat	size, sleeve inseam, chest, length
Pants	waist, length (inseam and outseam)
Shirt	collar, sleeve length
Shoe	size and width

Note: All men needing formalwear should have their measurements taken by a formalwear professional.

shirts and designer bow ties for the men in the wedding party, giving the ensemble a more personalized look. Or perhaps you can dispense with the ties entirely and instead have all the groomsmen wear shirts that do not require bow ties.

A tasteful selection of jewelry is another way to individualize a formal outfit, although when it comes to men's jewelry, I am a believer in "less is more." One or two nice pieces are all you need for your wedding. The man who sports more than a couple of items of jewelry can look overdone, no matter which expensive store the items came from. If you love jewelry, do yourself a favor and buy it for your wife.

The jewelry you wear must be chosen with care and taste. A fob watch on a chain, a beautiful wristwatch, or even a set of vintage cuff links can add impact to your wardrobe. A set of studs can be a great accent to your formal shirt, but if the studs make a bold statement, you should minimize your other accessories, or once again you'll risk a fussy, overproduced look.

When renting formal attire, it is seldom necessary to rent dress shoes. If one of your groomsmen doesn't have black patent-leather dress shoes, he probably has a pair of good, plain black calfskin shoes that will work perfectly well. Rental shoes seldom fit correctly, and comfort on your wedding day is far more important than whether everyone's shoes match precisely. With formalwear black silk socks will help give the men in your party a uniform look. If you are sporting new shoes at the wedding, wear them for a couple of weeks beforehand to break them in. Of course, all shoes—old, new, or rented—should be clean and well polished.

Whatever you decide to wear at your wedding, proper fit is critical. If you are buying a new garment, be sure to allow enough time for a final fitting after the tailoring has been done. Check the fit carefully in a three-way mirror, and bring your fiancée or best man along for a second pair of eyes. Look for the following in any suit or dinner jacket:

• The collar should cling to the back and sides of the neckline with no gaps or bulging.

• The coat should fit smoothly across the back and hug the shoulders snugly with no creases or areas of strain. Move your arms while the coat is buttoned to check comfort and how the jacket moves.

• The bottom hem of the jacket should cover your buttocks, and the vent or vents should not be pulled open.

• The sleeve should be hemmed at your wrist bone, allowing about half an inch of shirt to show. Lapels should lie flat with the jacket buttoned or unbuttoned.

• The trouser seat and crotch should follow the contours of your body. Remember to bring your wedding shoes to your fitting so that the tailor can hem the pants to the proper length.

The groom, his best man, and all other men in the wedding party generally dress alike or very similarly. Often the groom's outfit is distinguished from those of his ushers in one of the following ways:

• The groom's boutonniere has many blossoms, while his groomsmen wear single-blossoms.

• The groom wears a double-breasted tuxedo, while his groomsmen wear single-breasted tuxedos.

• The groom wears a three-piece suit, while his groomsmen wear matching suits without vest.

• The groom wears a one-button tuxedo, while his groomsmen wear three-button tuxedos.

• The groom's tuxedo has satin lapels, while those of his groomsmen are plain.

• The groom wears a bow tie with his suit, while his groomsmen wear standard ties.

• The groom wears a white dinner jacket, while his groomsmen sport traditional black tuxedos.

• The groom and groomsmen all wear the same color blazer, coordinating trousers, and bow ties, but the groom wears a different color tie.

• The groom wears a designer bow tie and coordinating vest or cummerbund with his tuxedo, while his groomsmen wear a plain black-tie ensemble without a vest or cummerbund.

What to Wear–and When

The following table is designed to show traditionally appropriate wedding attire for both grooms and groomsmen. While these are the traditions, I consider them only a guideline or point of reference. Under no circumstances should you feel locked into these examples if you wish to be more creative. For example, at his evening wedding, my friend Harry Hamlin looked handsome in an all-black ensemble: a plain black Gucci suit, black shirt, and standard black four-in-hand tie. It was an elegant and current look that ideally complemented the very simple Vera Wang wedding gown that his bride, Lisa, wore.

Please note that a "daytime" wedding occurs before six P.M.

Daytime Informal

Winter Dark business suit, navy blue blazer with khaki trousers, navy blue blazer with cream or white flannel trousers

Summer Light-colored suit *or* navy blazer with khaki, white, or cream linen trousers

Plain shirt with four-in-hand tie

Plain coordinating shoes

Daytime Semiformal

Black or dark gray sack coat, gray waistcoat

White pleated shirt or soft white shirt with standard four-in-hand tie

Plain black shoes

Daytime Formal

Black or gray morning coat ("cutaway") with black or gray striped trousers and gray waistcoat

Starched white shirt with turn-down collar with black-and-gray striped tie or dress ascot

Gray gloves

Black patent-leather dress shoes

Evening Informal

Winter Dark business suit *or* tuxedo, depending on bride's level of formality

Summer Navy or light-colored business suit *or* tuxedo, depending on bride's level of formality

Evening Semiformal

Winter Tuxedo

Summer Tuxedo or white dinner jacket with formal black trousers

White pleated shirt with turn-down collar

Black vest or cummerbund and matching bow tie or cravat

Black patent-leather dress shoes or plain black calfskin shoes

Evening Formal

"White tie and tails":

Black tailcoat and trousers, white piqué waistcoat

White starched-bosom shirt with wing collar

White bow tie

White gloves

Black-patent leather dress shoes

A Gentleman's Grooming

You'll be the center of attention on your wedding day, scrutinized by everyone, including parents, relatives, and maybe even a few of your old girlfriends. You'll also be the subject of literally hundreds of photos that you will look at for the rest of your life. Your wedding day is one time when you should take extra care with your appearance.

First of all, give yourself a long, hard look in a full-length mirror. Are you in good shape? Making a special effort to exercise regularly and watch your diet for at least a month before your wedding will pay off in how you look and feel. If you're a few pounds overweight, avoid junk food and focus on eating more nutritious, low-fat meals. Your wedding attire will fit better, you'll feel great, and you'll look trimmer in the photos. (Remember, the camera tends to add ten to fifteen pounds, and these are the pictures you are going to be looking at for a long time.)

Don't let yourself be worn down by all the celebrating before the wedding. The week before the big day, and particularly the night before, get to bed early. A good night's sleep is the best favor we can do ourselves in terms of our energy level and our appearance. You want to look and feel well rested, and the only way to do that is to get those eight hours of sleep!

Plan ahead and get a good haircut at least one week but no more than two weeks before your wedding day. This will give your hair a chance to grow a bit, avoiding that "just visited the barber" look. It's also a good idea to schedule your regular teeth cleaning with your oral hygienist for shortly before the wedding day, especially if you are a heavy smoker or coffee drinker.

The week before the wedding, pamper yourself. If you have never had a professional facial, now would be a great time. Because facials can sometimes cause temporary skin redness, schedule it at least a week before the wedding. Many men have a monthly facial as part of their regular grooming routine. You'll be amazed how clean and fresh your skin will look after a good facial. Also, if you have a beard or mustache, consider a visit to a barber for a professional trim, and have any unsightly nasal or ear hair clipped as well.

Take time for a professional manicure the day before the wedding. Nothing completes the picture of a well-groomed man like trimmed and buffed nails. I think it's also a wonderful idea for the groom to splurge for a manicurist to do the nails of your groomsmen. Once the good-natured kidding has stopped, you'll find the guys love the pampering just as much as the ladies–who, I'll guarantee, have already scheduled their own manicures and pedicures. Coordinate with your bride, if you like, for one or two on-site manicurists to handle the entire wedding party. And before you head out to the ceremony, rub in a little hand cream so that your hands will feel smooth during those dozens of con-gratulatory handshakes.

On your wedding day, first thing in the morning, try to get in some vigorous exercise. It will help ease any tension you may be feeling, and if it's sunny outside, it will give you some color and better skin tone. I also recommend having a professional massage for both you and your bride on the morning of your wedding. The wedding day is high-pressure, and massage will make you feel relaxed and energized.

Be sure not to eat garlic or other aromatic foods for twenty-four hours before your wedding; it's amazing how these odors can linger on the breath and in perspiration. On the morning of the wedding, use mouthwash after brushing your teeth. You might also pop a miniature bottle of breath freshener or breath mints in a pocket. A splash of cologne is also a nice touch. If you don't have a favorite scent, visit a good department store well in advance of your wedding and try a few types until you find one that you like. Just be sure not to use too heavy a hand with the cologne on your wedding day; you want a pleasant scent, not an overpowering one.

If your wedding is scheduled for late in the day, wait to shave until about an hour before you get dressed. Two shaves in a day can sometimes irritate your skin, and the second shave is never as close as the first. Have the best man check you over carefully to make sure you haven't missed any

Dressing

Many grooms have to dress for their wedding in an unfamiliar setting, such as a hotel room. If you must pack up your wedding attire, it is critical to double-check that you have everything so that you don't find yourself without an essential item at the last minute. You cannot believe how many times it's been an hour before the ceremony, and I've found a groomsman—or sometimes even the groom—missing trousers, shoes, or socks!

The best way to be sure you have everything is to go through the process of dressing from the ground up—in your mind. Start with your shoes, socks, briefs, trousers, and so on up to your collar stays and tie. Do this twice. Don't omit easy-to-forget items such as cuff links or studs. If you think you might have a tendency to forget something in the last-minute excitement, make a checklist of all the elements in your wedding ensemble, and pack them the day before, when you can be more focused and less rushed.

Groom's Checklist

Shoes

Socks

Briefs

Undershirt

Trousers

Shirt

Collar stays

Cuff links and studs

Coat or jacket

Vest

Cummerbund or belt

Tie

Watch

Bride's wedding ring

spots and that your hair is evenly trimmed. Don't forget a dab of moisturizer on your face to improve the look of your skin. There are some very good tinted men's moisturizers available now that add just a bit of color so you look your best in photos and videos. You also may want to consider men's cosmetics, such as bronzer or a dusting of face powder, as another option. Try out bronzers and colors before your wedding day to ensure a natural not-made-up look.

Don't try to grab a quick tan the day before or the morning of your wedding. I can't tell you how many times I've seen grooms who showed up at the altar looking like a lobster. Not only are they uncomfortable, but they look beet red in all the wedding photos. If you do want to pick up a *little* color, and I emphasize a *little*, be sure to use a good sunscreen with a sun protection factor (SPF) of between 6 and 15, depending on how sun-sensitive you are. All in all, a bit of bronzer is a much safer approach and will make you look just as good.

Great Ideas for Boutonnieres

Sprig of lilac

Stephanotis

Spray of freesia

Rose with eucalyptus leaves

Spray of lily of the valley

Sprig of colorful grape hyacinth

Chapter 11

The Bachelor Party

Tasteful Versus Tacky

Mention "bachelor party" to most brides, and they'll roll their eyes. "I don't want to know," they'll say, finding some solace in denial.

Indeed, the specter of the bachelor party strikes fear into the hearts of most brides, who assume their fiancé will be led down the path of evil by his fellow friends. These fears are hardly unfounded, as most stag parties follow a fairly typical format, at least according to legend and as evidenced by some I've had the misfortune to witness:

1. The groom and his buddies spend an evening ingesting prodigious amounts of alcohol and attempting to outdo one another in out-of-control behavior.

2. There may be a paid appearance by a dancer, who will perform one or more of the following practices: jumping out of a cake, a striptease, lap dancing, or something involving whipped cream that you definitely would not want your bride-to-be to know about.

3. Everyone will drive home blind drunk at three A.M., endangering themselves and others on the road.

4. Everyone will wake up with a head-splitting hangover and spend the following day regretting their behavior. Or the worst-case scenario: The wedding is the next day, and the green-faced groom stands at the altar hoping he won't pass out.

Let's be honest: The "typical" party doesn't sound like fun. It sounds more like some nightmarish 1950s frat party gone awry.

The old concept of the bachelor party is really inappropriate. In the past, when young people led more sheltered lives, the bachelor party was the one time a group of young men could kick up their heels and raise hell. There was little stigma about drunkenness and almost no awareness of the dangers of driving while intoxicated. In this day and age we are frightfully aware of the harmful effects of overindulgence in alcohol. None of us need to do that to our bodies or risk endangering ourselves and others by driving drunk. And somehow paying a woman to strip and perform acts for a dozen of your friends doesn't quite seem like the harmless bit of fun it might have twenty years ago. It's disrespectful to your fiancée, who would definitely find it distasteful if she knew, and it doesn't exactly sound like appropriate behavior for a gentleman, either.

I urge grooms to find other ways of celebrating the last few days of bachelorhood. After all, what's important is sharing time and reminiscences with your closest friends, which can be done in a variety of settings that are conducive to having a great party, without falling into the conventional stag party trap of getting drunk and possibly doing something that you might have otherwise have had the common sense to avoid–something you might spend the rest of your life regretting.

The key thing is not to be waylaid by a raffish best man who wants to take you to the Chicken Ranch in Las Vegas. Well beforehand sit down with your best man and discuss your ideas for a get-together with the guys. Insist that you do not want the typical outdated bachelor party for your celebration. He'll get the picture right away and may be relieved that he doesn't have to run around sourcing ladies of the evening or be embarrassed when they do show.

Different Kinds of Bachelor Parties

Think about what you *really* want to do. For a group of friends who like to fish, nothing could be more fun than a fishing weekend at a riverside cabin in the wilderness. Pack in plenty of food, along with a few cases of fine local microbrews, good cigars, and some great wines to complement the catch. You can't help but have a wonderful couple of days.

Explore the idea of an overnight trip to a favorite nearby destination, such as a resort town or a city with great restaurants. Reserve some rooms at a nice hotel, including one suite where your friends can all hang out and party. Get a reservation at an informal Mexican or Middle Eastern restaurant for a relaxing evening of eating, drinking, and laughing. The next day enjoy brunch together, play a round of golf, and hit the spa for a steam and shower before returning home. Rent a van and driver to make the trip part of the fun.

If you and your groomsmen share an interest in a sport, such as skiing, surfing, or tennis, you can build a weekend around it. A ski weekend in a rented lodge can be a great bachelor weekend. Spring for private lessons from the resort's experts for a nice touch. Or pack your boards and get away to a beach with prime surfing conditions. Dinner together at a restaurant overlooking the waves will be a chance to unwind and swap surfing stories, eat fresh fish, and enjoy the change in scenery.

For the bachelor party of a friend of mine, we rented a houseboat on Lake Mead for a weekend. One of my friends, who's really into top-class scotch, brought a half case of his favorites so we could start the evening with a single-malt tasting, which was enlightening as well as fun. The weather was stunning, the experience incredibly relaxing, and all the guys tried to outdo each other as the barbecue chef du jour, making for some pretty tasty dining.

Maybe you don't have an entire weekend to spend, but you love the great outdoors. Map out a challenging hiking trail and take to the woods with your buddies for the day. Be well prepared, Boy Scout style, with plenty of water, a first-aid kit, and the proper clothing. Afterward, you can kick back–and nurse any sore muscles–at a ranch-style steakhouse, indulging in a few bottles of fine Napa

Valley cabernet sauvignon.

Another idea is to build your bachelor party around a performance, like a concert by a favorite rock band or an evening of jazz at a local club. Have dinner together at a great restaurant beforehand, then enjoy the music. Top things off with a nightcap at the hottest bar in town.

If you or your best man has the space in your home, you can also invite your friends over for a great party. Time it around a long-anticipated televised sporting event for a classic evening of male bonding. If you'll all be drinking, designate a driver, spring for taxis, or let everybody sleep over.

My final piece of advice is very, very important. Never schedule your bachelor party for the night before your wedding. Yes, I know, you don't intend to overindulge, but why risk it? It is best to hold your bachelor party the weekend before the wedding. The days right before the wedding will be full enough without adding this event (and the possibility of a hangover) to the calendar.

How to Prevent a Hangover

Let's say you do go out for an evening of drinking with the guys. There are several preventive measures (aside from not overindulging in the first place) that you can take to stave off the effects of alcohol. First, be sure to have a substantial lunch and dinner before you head out. Second, stick with one type of drink; mixing gin, tequila, and wine is asking for trouble. Third, drink gallons of water throughout the evening. Take a break between each drink, and have at least one full glass of water during the downtime. Finally, when you arrive home–we are presuming you were driven there by a sober driver–again drink several glasses of water. Take two aspirin. Pop a few vitamin B_{12} and vitamin C tablets. Pull down the shades, turn the ringer off the phone, turn off the alarm, and go right to bed. Don't forget to pray a lot–you may need it!

How to Handle a Hellacious Hangover

The pounding head, the shaking hands, the queasy stomach–there's nothing like the pain of a killer hangover to make one regret the night before. Hopefully you'll learn a lesson from this punishing experience, but in the meantime there is a secret remedy that may make you feel alive again. Reportedly it was developed by a Swiss physician. It is incredibly nutritious. It's also highly restorative if you are sick. A friend of mine who was extremely ill lived on this for two months, and it was the only thing he could keep down. I have tried it many times, and it works!

The recipe is as follows: Steam some green beans, zucchini, celery, and parsley until the vegetables are crisp and tender. Drain the vegetables, reserving the water. Purée the vegetables in a blender with a little of the steaming water to liquify it, and add a pinch of salt. It should be about the consistency of a soup. Drink it, and you will instantly start to feel better. Then again, it probably isn't possible to feel any worse!

OMSMAN *Father of the*
BRIDE

BRIDESMAID

Moth
BR

Chapter 12

The Rehearsal Dinner

The rehearsal dinner is traditionally held the evening before the wedding and usually follows a rehearsal of the ceremony involving the entire wedding party. The dinner used to be reserved for the wedding party only, but it is now customary for the guest list to include both sets of parents; the adult attendants and their spouses, companions, or dates; the parents of any children in the wedding party; and the officiant or officiants who presided at the ceremony rehearsal. Often close relatives of the bride and groom are invited, as are guests from out of town.

Frequently the groom's family is responsible for the planning and hosting of the rehearsal dinner, so this may be an event where you are called upon to practice your skills as a host. Because it is a more intimate setting than the wedding to follow, this dinner can be a wonderful opportunity for your family to get to know the bride's family and your close friends.

If your family is hosting the rehearsal dinner, invitations for the event can be sent from your family and mailed separately from the wedding invitation or they can be included as an insert in the wedding invitation itself. If the rehearsal dinner invitations are being mailed separately, they need not follow the format or style of the wedding invitations, but they should suit the type of party planned, whether it be a semiformal get-together in the private room of a favorite restaurant or a casual backyard barbecue. Invitations to the rehearsal dinner should be mailed at about the same time as the wedding invitations so that any out-of-town guests can make their travel plans accordingly.

If the rehearsal dinner immediately follows the actual rehearsal of the wedding ceremony, the dinner should be held at a location that is convenient to the rehearsal site. If guests who are not involved in the rehearsal are invited to the dinner, they should be invited for a time that is approximately when you expect the rehearsal to end. Because it is possible that no one from the wedding party will be at the rehearsal dinner to greet early-arriving guests, be sure to designate a close friend or relative to act as temporary host, greeting the guests and making them feel comfortable until you, your fiancée, and your parents arrive.

If there are many people at the rehearsal dinner who don't know one another, it's up to you and the bride to make a special effort to introduce everyone. It's also best to plan the seating in advance and use place cards. Assigned seating enables you to place guests together who should meet one another, or who already may know one another, or who may have something in common. Tented place cards with the names on both the front and the back allow everyone at a table to easily read the names of other guests at the table. Be particularly aware of family tensions and politics, and separate those who would not care to be seated near each other.

There really are no rules for the rehearsal dinner except that it should in no way upstage the wedding reception. This is not the occasion for elaborate decor and a lavish multicourse dinner. A less formal get-together is not only more appropriate, it will help everyone get better acquainted before the wedding.

One thing to remember is to coordinate your attire for the dinner with your bride. Your respective outfits shouldn't match, but they should complement each other and be at the same level of formality or informality.

The rehearsal dinner is a good time for you and your bride to present your gifts to your attendants, which can be done in front of the guests, with appreciative testimonials from you and your bride, or privately, whichever you prefer. The rehearsal dinner is also a convenient time for you to give any checks for services, such as the officiant's fee or the balance due to the band, to the best man for handling the following day.

Because the rehearsal dinner involves the people who are closest to you, it is a wonderful opportunity for toasting and reminiscences during the course of the evening. Be sure your family and the members of your wedding party understand that long-winded toasts and risqué stories should be reserved for the rehearsal dinner, not the wedding. You can get the ball rolling with a toast–and perhaps a few stories–in your parents' honor. If you suspect that people may be shy about getting up, take a few key guests aside in advance and ask them if they would like to speak. And since this occasion may provide some priceless moments during the toasts and speeches, you may want to have it captured on video. Or maybe not!

Most of all the rehearsal dinner should be fun and relaxed. Here are some ideas for gatherings that will get your wedding celebration off to a great start.

• Plan an evening at a local winery, including a wine tasting, with dinner overlooking the vineyards.

• Take over a private room at your favorite Greek restaurant and hire a band for traditional Greek dancing and plate breaking after dinner.

• Hold a Texas-style barbecue in the barn of a local farm, with plenty of ribs, chili, and beer.

• Have your dinner in the private room of a Middle Eastern restaurant featuring a menu of classic fare such as hummus, baba ghanoush, and lamb kebabs.(Belly dancer optional!)

• If you're near the beach, have a catered New England-style clambake featuring clams, lobster, potatoes, and homemade key lime pie and watermelon for dessert.

• Hold a casual buffet dinner at your country club in a room overlooking the golf course.

• Book a private room at the best Chinese restaurant in town, and give your guests the experience of a multicourse, family-style Chinese dinner.

• Take over your favorite Mexican restaurant, and offer a great south-of-the-border buffet with a salsa bar and mariachi music.

- If a hotel is the best location for your rehearsal dinner, perhaps there's an interesting and fun location on the hotel grounds other than a typical private room; maybe around the hotel pool or in a room that opens onto a terrace or lawn.

Two last words of advice. Keep an eye on the alcohol, and instruct your bartenders to pour moderately. You don't want the wedding party to be too wasted and suffer from hangovers on your wedding day. And to help the members of the wedding get plenty of rest for the following day, don't let the event drag on to the wee hours. If the party's going strong, make sure you and your bride sneak away early enough to enjoy a good night's sleep. Instruct your best man to drag you off and drive you home if need be. You'll thank him in the morning.

Chapter 13

Ensuring a Romantic Wedding Day

When a bride and groom are involved in the myriad preparations for their wedding day, it is sometimes difficult to remember that at its most basic, this day is about you and your fiancée. I always remind grooms that no matter how frantic the day seems and how many people are crowding around, it is important to focus in on your bride and on ways you can make the day extra special for her.

So many brides have told me that their sweetest memories of their wedding day were of something their groom did to show his love. I've suggested this idea to many grooms, and it's always worked well. One bride was in her dressing room with her bridesmaids just minutes before the ceremony, when there was a knock on the door. She opened it to find the best man holding an envelope. Sitting down, the bride read the most heartfelt love letter she had ever received from her groom. He wrote of his abiding love for her, his happiness on their wedding day, and his hopes for the future. She couldn't hold back her tears, but she was incredibly radiant when she walked down the aisle.

Another bride was sequestered with her mother when the florist delivered a small box that had been completely appliquéd with pale green leaves and tied with a white satin ribbon. The bride opened the leaf-covered box to find a note from her husband-to-be and, to her surprise, a jeweler's case containing a gorgeous diamond-and-pearl pendant to be attached to the string of pearls she was wearing. "You are the pearl of my life, and I will always cherish you," the note read. "Love, Gordon."

Remember that in general women are much more emotional than men, and I am sure your bride would love to receive a special romantic gesture from you on your wedding day. I recommend you think carefully about her and how you want to express your love to her. A gift with a romantic note is a touching way to show your feelings. Because your gift will be so special, it should be presented in a dramatic way. A special box, such as the leaf-covered container created by the florist mentioned earlier, can give your gift added beauty and impact. Think about the things that are most meaningful to your bride and how you can incorporate those elements into a gift or its packaging. If she loves antiques, perhaps you can find a beautiful vintage snuffbox to hold a pair of pearl drop earrings. If she is an outdoor type who adores hiking in the mountains, your florist might cover a box with birch bark, line it with moss, and tie it with raffia to hold a special gift.

Jewelry is a traditional gift from the groom to the bride on their wedding day. Classically styled pieces that will stand the test of time are best, unless your bride collects jewelry of a certain era or type. Having the piece engraved with your initials or a message of love is a romantic touch that will make the gift even more special. I love vintage jewelry and think it's ideal for the bride's gift, because the pieces have a history and yet seem timeless. The possibilities are virtually endless, but here are some ideas.

String of pearls

Pendant for pearl necklace

Pearl bracelet

Heirloom piece of jewelry from your family

Vintage watch, engraved with message from you

Gold charm bracelet, with first charm from you

Pearl drop earrings

Vintage pin

If your bride doesn't care for jewelry but you would like to present her with a special gift, most fine jewelers carry a selection of sterling silver items that can be engraved and personalized, such as a pillbox or other small box, compact, or key ring. You might also take a favorite photograph of the two of you and have it set in a sterling silver frame engraved with both of your initials.

But there is no reason to feel obligated to give your bride an expensive gift on your wedding day. I always say that the most important part of the bridegroom's gift to the bride is the note that accompanies it. These words and emotions from you will mean more to your bride than the biggest jewel on the planet. So take the time to write a beautiful note that expresses your feelings on your wedding day, and have it delivered to your bride moments before the ceremony. Needless to say, this is something you should script well in advance, because you may not be at your most articulate during the hours before your wedding ceremony. The note can be pages long, just a few words, or a piece of poetry, but it should come from your heart. Write the note on your computer, if that's easier, and then copy it in your handwriting when you are satisfied with the wording. Some grooms have written a beautiful love poem to their bride, which can be kept private between the couple or read at the ceremony if desired.

You can make your note extra special by writing it on beautiful handmade paper or using other unusual materials. If your handwriting is poor, think about having the calligrapher who made your place cards transfer your words to paper in elegant script.

Still another option that comes to mind is what one bride did for her groom as they waited out the minutes before the ceremony in their separate dressing areas. We had a video camera set up in the bride's dressing room, and a VCR in the groom's dressing area. During a quiet moment the bride taped a short video in which she spoke of her love for her groom, her feelings on their wedding day, and her hopes for the future. We delivered it to the groom, who watched the surprise tape just before he took his place for the ceremony. He was very touched by the loving words of his soon-to-be-wife.

Here's what one bridegroom, Rick Otto, wrote for his bride, Vanessa Angel. He read it to her during their ceremony.

Beloved Wife

Thinking of you
on this our special day
all of our dreams
our life together
beginning
walking hand in hand
down the aisle
through the fields of life
towards the mountains
our journey
having begun
as we grow and love
unconditionally
completely
our hearts
now one
loving you Vanessa
my wife
loving you

Chapter 14

The Ceremony

So many grooms think there's a "one size fits all" wedding ceremony, but that's not the case. Your wedding ceremony should be uniquely yours. These are the words that will unite you and your bride in front of all your family and friends; your vows should be given as much thought as the rest of your wedding arrangements, and the ritual should fit you as perfectly as your wedding suit.

Whether you want a five-minute civil ceremony in front of a judge or a traditional Jewish religious ritual conducted by a rabbi, your ceremony should be an expression of your values and beliefs. These are your personal vows and no one else's.

Early on you should sit down with your fiancée and discuss your preferences for your wedding ritual. If both of you are from the same religious and social background, you may easily agree on the type of ceremony. But that situation seems to occur less and less frequently today, as there are more interracial, interfaith, and intercultural marriages than ever before. Ceremonies that reflect this diversity can be very meaningful.

Overall, there are four common types of ceremonies:

• Religious: Filled with the beliefs and rituals of faith, the ceremony is performed by a priest, minister, rabbi, or other ordained official.

• Interfaith: When individuals of different faiths are joined in marriage, the ceremony may be performed by two officiants, one from each faith, or

The Wedding Rituals of Several Major Religions and How They Differ

The Catholic Ceremony

Couples who marry in the Catholic Church are often required to attend premarital counseling to be sure they are prepared for marriage. The Catholic wedding ceremony is usually but not always performed within the context of a nuptial mass. The mass begins with the bridal procession, and the bride and groom stand, kneel, or sit in front of the altar throughout the service. The Catholic Church does permit the mass to be personalized by having friends or family give readings or sing hymns. The mass includes Holy Communion, which is administered to Roman Catholics in the congregation.

The Protestant Ceremony

Protestant ceremonies differ depending on the denomination: Lutheran, Methodist, Episcopal, Baptist, and so on. Still, all Protestant ceremonies contain the same major elements: the procession of the bridal party, the introduction by the minister, the vows by the couple and the exchange of rings, and the recession. Protestant ceremonies can be very short, or they can be lengthened with readings from the Old or New Testament, other readings, music, or the taking of Holy Communion.

The Jewish Ceremony

The Jewish wedding ceremony is rich in symbolism, from the *chuppah* (canopy), which represents the newlyweds' new home, to the breaking of the glass by the bridegroom, which symbolizes the destruction of the temple in Jerusalem in 70 B.C. The service will vary depending on whether it is Orthodox (the most traditional and strict), Conservative (somewhat less strict), or Reform (the most liberal), but it will usually include the following elements. The bride, groom, and their attendants enter in procession and gather under the *chuppah*. Sometimes the couple's parents join in the procession and gather under or behind the *chuppah*. The bridal couple partakes of a sip of wine, then is blessed by the rabbi. The groom gives the bride a plain gold wedding ring, and the *ketubah*, or marriage contract, is read out loud. The seven marriage benedictions are recited, often by a family member or close friend, followed by another sip of wine for the bride and groom. The ceremony ends with the ritual crushing of the glass by the groom and wishes of *Mazel tov!* or *best wishes* from the congregation. Most Jewish ceremonies are performed in Hebrew and English.

The Muslim (Islamic) Ceremony

The Muslim wedding tradition is very different from those of the Christian and Jewish faiths; in fact, there is no Western-style "wedding" at all. Instead, the union of the bride and groom is a private matter, where the *mahr*, or dowry the groom gives the bride, is negotiated ahead of time and formalized before an Islamic magistrate in an office with three male witnesses in attendance. Often this signing of the wedding contract is followed by more public celebrations that happen several weeks later. There can be a succession of parties, which follow traditional guidelines and may include ancient, symbolic rituals.

by one officiant who is familiar with both religions.

• Secular or civil: In a civil service a judge officiates, using a nonsectarian text.

• Spiritual: Increasingly popular, spiritual ceremonies emphasize humanistic values rather than a religious belief system.

Personalizing your Ceremony

Today most officiants permit the bride and groom to incorporate elements into their wedding ritual that express their personalities and values. Writing your own vows, asking close friends or relatives to give readings, incorporating poetry or music, having a friend with a wonderful voice sing a favorite song or aria, or involving the entire congregation in lighting unity candles are all ways of tailoring your ceremony to fit your vision and personality. The music you choose for the procession, the ceremony itself, and the recession doesn't have to be the standard wedding music, either. It could be spirituals, rock tunes, or romantic ballads. I encourage brides and grooms to enhance their ceremony by adding elements that are important and meaningful to them personally. It will make your wedding unique and memorable. Printing the text of readings, poems, songs, or an aria in the ceremony program for the guests to keep is a nice touch.

Remember, the choice of officiant or officiants is a major decision. This individual will join you and your bride in marriage, so he or she should be someone with whom you have a rapport and who is receptive to your input. Be sure the officiant understands and supports the style and tone of ceremony you have in mind. Ask to review the standard text and find out exactly what the officiant intends to say during the ceremony. You should be able to edit or rewrite the text to make it suit you and your bride. This is your ceremony and you should be comfortable with all the statements and wording.

If your family has strong feelings about the type of ceremony you wish, it is important to voice these feelings early to your fiancée and her family. A wedding is a blending of families, not a situation where one family runs the show. Creating a ceremony that interweaves the personalities and backgrounds of the bride and groom can be a rewarding experience that brings the two families closer together. Some of the most moving ceremonies I have attended have been ones that highlighted and celebrated the different heritage of the bride, the groom, and their families.

With interfaith ceremonies, it is thoughtful to offer guests a ceremony program that explains the meaning of the rituals of each religion. This will help guests to understand the different elements of the service. This program can be rolled into a scroll and tied with ribbon or raffia, if desired, for a more attractive presentation. Before the ceremony the program may be placed on the chairs or pews or handed to guests as they enter.

Should you plan on giving your own readings, be sure to make several copies of your selection and entrust one to the best man in case you misplace yours. I was once at a wedding where the bride and groom had literally spent hours writing the vows they were to speak to each other, and in the last-minute flurry they left the text at home.

The Greek Orthodox Ceremony

Another ceremony rich in ritual, the Greek Orthodox wedding service begins with the betrothal of the bride and groom, when the couple is blessed and rings are exchanged. The high point of the ceremony occurs when the bride and groom are crowned, with crowns that are usually attached to each other by ribbon. In the Greek Orthodox religion this is meant to symbolize the bride and groom's "coronation" into a new family. Scriptures are read; the bride and groom take a sip of wine; and the priest and the couple's "sponsor," a person important to the couple, leads them three times around the altar. At the end of the ceremony the priest blesses the couple, and there is a recession.

Breaking the Glass

In the Jewish faith it is traditional at the end of the marriage ceremony for the groom to stamp on a wineglass wrapped in a napkin, breaking it. Some say the glass is broken to remind the congregation of the destruction of the temple in Jerusalem; others say it symbolizes the fragility of life. Whatever the meaning, the breaking of the glass is always a moment of great joy in a Jewish ceremony. To make sure no mishap mars the occasion, I don't use a drinking glass but instead substitute a standard lightbulb, placed in a zip-top plastic bag and wrapped in a napkin. The lightbulb always breaks easily; it makes a nice, satisfying breaking sound, and there's less danger of anyone being cut by the glass.

Most churches and synagogues have rules and regulations about what is and is not permitted in sanctuaries; in some cases the rules are strict. It is important to find out early on what the rules are at the facility you have selected, to make sure you can have the ceremony you wish. If real difficulties arise, it may be best to look for an alternate location.

If you've chosen your attendants well, your best man and groomsmen can be a great source of support for you at the ceremony. It's your best man's job to make sure you get to the ceremony site on time, stand in the right spot, and offer the ring at the proper moment. He can also provide a bit of welcome distraction by chatting with you as the minutes tick off prior to the bride's entrance.

Stage fright is absolutely normal for grooms. In fact, you'd be pretty unusual if you didn't feel any butterflies at the start of your ceremony. The key thing is learning how not to *look* nervous, an art practiced by accomplished public speakers and seasoned actors. Almost all of them get nervous, but they are trained not to show it.

The first trick? Knowing your lines. Days before the ceremony, spend time by yourself and practice saying your vows in a clear, loud voice. I know, it sounds unromantic, but knowing the material will help it seem less scary. You also won't have to concentrate as much on what you're saying and can instead enjoy the moment.

Another way to stay relaxed is to stand up straight and try to breathe regularly and normally. Remember that you're surrounded by people who love you—you couldn't have a more supportive audience.

No matter how nervous you may feel, resist any temptation to pop a tranquilizer or toss back a stiff belt of booze before the ceremony. I know a bride and groom who seemed to sleepwalk through the ceremony and later confessed they each took one half of a tranquilizer and barely remember any part of their wedding day. Don't anesthetize yourself—you want to "be there" with a clear head for this all-important day.

The Rehearsal

Unless you are having a five-minute civil ceremony, the rehearsal is no mere formality. Gathering the entire wedding party and walking through the steps of the ceremony with the officiant will help ensure that everyone is familiar with the ritual and their role in it. It will also allow you to fine-tune timing and make sure all the elements you have planned work well together. Have the ceremony music on hand so that you can walk through the procession and recession with the music playing to make sure that the pieces are the appropriate length. Tell everyone involved that they should arrive on time and that elements of the ceremony may be practiced two or three times until you and your fiancée are satisfied that everything will go smoothly when the day arrives.

Chapter 15

The Ultimate Party

Making it Personal

You may have taken a backseat in the planning of your wedding reception and let your bride take the lead, but guess what? You and your bride are the host and hostess! You, the groom, play a unique role at your reception, because the entire event revolves around you and your bride. In a very real sense you are the host at this gathering, and it's important that you understand what is expected of you.

Often the bride and groom spend the first part of the reception at a photography session, with the rest of the wedding party. I urge you to keep this photo session short. It is seldom necessary for anyone to have an endless series of formal photos of various combinations of wedding-party members. Candid photos of you, your friends, and your relatives enjoying yourselves at the reception are much more fun. Plus, the less time you spend in photography, the more time you'll have with your guests at the reception. Remember that each formal photo takes about three minutes, so if you plan on doing twenty shots, you'll spend an hour–which may be too much time to spend capturing a day that you're missing out on!

After the photos are done, if your reception follows the traditional format, there will be a moment when the bandleader, emcee, or the best man announces your entrance. From that moment on the energy of the evening centers around the two of you. If you and your bride are in the room, the party sparkles. If you leave the reception or get caught up at one table for a prolonged period of time, the party can quickly go flat.

Since you are the hosts, you and your bride should plan on making a special effort during the evening to visit as many tables as possible, either separately or together, to greet your guests and thank them for coming. At a very large wedding it may not be possible to get around to all the tables, but you should do your best.

One approach that works very well is for the bride and groom to be introduced as soon as the guests have taken their seats and immediately proceed to the dance floor for their first dance. It gets the party off to a rousing start, and a good twenty-five minutes of dancing makes a great segue from cocktails to reception. But every couple should do what they feel will work for them; you don't have to dance at all if you don't care to. At Kenny G's wedding, there was no dancing, just great music played all evening as guests dined on a gourmet meal.

When guests have been seated, it is traditional for the father of the bride to welcome the guests and

Toasts

You are hardly on your own when it comes to thinking up the appropriate toast. Don't feel you must be completely original; there are plenty of great resources that list a variety of toasts, including books on the specific subject of wedding toasts. The Internet is also a good source; just search for "wedding toasts," and you will come up with hundreds of ideas. I do think the best toasts are those you write yourself, because they are the most sincere and personal. Keep it short, sweet, and from your heart, and you'll do fine.

I found this good advice in a charity auction catalog, from an anonymous source who obviously knew his toasting. "For a toast to sound as if it just came to you in an affectionate flash, it will have to be prepared ahead of time. Know your message, how to open, and how to close. A quote is always nice. Be cheery, to the point, short, and sweet. Mean what you say. If a toast isn't from the heart, it means nothing at all."

Toasts Around the World

A votre santé! "To your health," in French

Viva l'amor! "Long live love," in Italian

Hanya! "To good health," in Arabic

Mazel tov! "Good luck" or "best wishes," in Hebrew

L'chayim! "To life," in Hebrew

Op je gezondheid! "To your health," in Dutch

make a toast to the bride and groom. Often the best man follows with his toast. At a large wedding the bride's father, the best man, and other toasters should step to the band's microphone so that they can be heard by all the guests. Your best man should be asked to keep his toast short and sweet, as indeed all toasting should be at a wedding. The bride and groom's turn to make a toast, if they wish, is at the cake cutting. It's a good idea to write out your toast in advance and practice it until you have it memorized. It looks more spontaneous if you don't have to check an index card for your next line!

At many weddings dancing begins quite early in the party, often before the meal has been served. You should plan with your bride when the dancing will occur and communicate your desired timing to your wedding planner and to the bandleader. Usually the bride and groom proceed to the floor for the first dance to a favorite song. I recommend taking a few brush-up dancing lessons before the wedding so that you can dance with confidence.

After the bride and groom dance, it is traditional for the bride to dance with her father and for you to ask her mother to dance. I usually delay the father-daughter dance until after dinner is served, because it is a great way to start the next dance set. You can also ask the best man to cut in on the bride at a certain juncture, leaving you free to dance with your own mother or another woman in the wedding party. Typically the gentlemen at a wedding will vie for a chance to dance with the bride, so this is one time you should not monopolize her, although you should catch her eye frequently to see if she needs "rescuing."

The Finale

The cutting of the wedding cake by the bride and groom is one of the high points of the festivities. Since this is a major photo opportunity, you might want to sneak out and run a comb through your hair beforehand. I have also found that the groom's boutonniere tends to look pretty tired toward the middle of the evening, after it's been crushed by all the hugging and kissing. Have your florist provide a second boutonniere so that you can switch to the fresh one before the cake cutting.

The bandleader will generally announce the cutting of the cake or play music to get the guests' attention. Be sure you and your bride are properly positioned for photography before you actually make the first cut. Traditionally the groom feeds his bride the first bite of cake, and then she reciprocates. In recent years an unsavory practice has sprung up of pushing cake into the bride's face. This is a mean-spirited, awful custom, and I personally find it distasteful. No one wants cake all over their face, ever, least of all when they have spent hours getting ready for one of the most joyous days of their lives.

The groom's big moment–the garter toss–is a custom that is occurring less and less frequently. According to wedding legend, the bachelor lucky enough to catch it will be the next to marry.

A word of advice: Don't party until dawn. Enjoy some dancing after the cake cutting, and then make a graceful exit. You should leave while the party is in full swing and at its highest peak of energy. If you leave at a sensible hour instead of frolicking until dawn, you'll also be in better shape for a romantic post nuptial interlude.

Table Talk

One long-standing tradition at weddings is for the bride and groom and their parents or members of the wedding party to be seated at a long, elevated table facing the guests. I think this looks as though the happy couple and their friends are in a shop window or in a debate! Also, the bride, groom, and members of the wedding party are frequently up and about during the evening, leaving a long, empty, spotlighted table with perhaps two people at it–which looks as though everyone important has left the party. I prefer to place the bride and groom at a round or oval table, same as the rest of the guests, in the center of the action, seated with members of the wedding party. It looks much more natural, particularly when the wedding party are up dancing or greeting guests at other tables.

Party Planning

The way you arrange the space for your reception can make the difference between a great party and a dull one. I prefer to put the dance floor in the center of the room, keeping it as the center of energy. The bride and groom's table goes next to the dance floor in a central location. Even if the space is huge, I cluster guests' tables as close together as possible for more intimacy and energy. When tables are widely spaced, guests hardly feel like they're at a party. The energy dissipates rather than flowing from table to table. I also put the wedding cake in a prominent position, illuminated by lights so that the cake is a focal point. Most wedding cakes are elaborate creations of the baker's art and they deserve to be front and center during the entire party, not just moved into the spotlight when it's time for the cake-cutting.

Chapter 16

On Your Wedding Night

The moment you've both been waiting for is here—your first night together as a married couple. One of the biggest secrets about marriage is that the wedding night is often anti-climactic, even disappointing. Many happily married couples have confessed to me that their wedding night was a dud. After the excitement and stress of their wedding day and vast amounts of champagne, some couples are simply too exhausted for a night of connubial bliss. Others have built up the experience in their mind to a point where even good sex would be a letdown. I've seen studies that revealed up to half of all married couples didn't have sex on their wedding night.

But don't worry. You and your bride may decide that you're too tired after your long day in the spotlight, and you'd rather reserve the consummation of your marriage for the following morning or evening. But perhaps you would like to make your wedding night special and ensure that the environment is as relaxing and romantic as you can make it.

In any case the setting for your first night as a married couple is important. Even if the wedding is held at your in-laws' home, I advise not staying under the parental roof on your wedding night. It's not very romantic. The optimal environment is a luxurious hotel room, ideally a presidential or honeymoon suite. If you are hosting your wedding reception at a hotel and book well in advance, the management will often upgrade your standard room to the honeymoon suite at no additional charge. Honeymoon suites generally are spacious and have extra amenities such as a whirlpool tub or a fireplace. A honeymoon suite may sound like an extravagance, but for a typical wedding it is quite practical. The extra space of a suite may be needed if the bride is dressing there with her mother and bridesmaids.

But a hotel suite, no matter how luxurious, is somewhat impersonal. There are dozens of ways that you can transform this neutral space into an intimate setting for romance. Call ahead to determine what amenities your room has. Then make arrangements with the concierge to fill the room with things that your bride loves. Appeal to all her senses: sight, sound, smell, taste, and touch. A framed photo of the two of you might go on the bedside table. Ask to rent a compact disc player or bring a portable one if the room has none, and arrange a selection of her favorite CDs—or several you have purchased for the occasion—next to it. Arrange hundreds of candles on every surface, drape a silken throw on the bed, and lay a fire in the fireplace.

Then only the final touches are needed, which can be provided by the concierge or innkeeper while you are at the reception. Have the hot tub filled with scented water and set to bubbling. Chill a bottle of fine French champagne in a silver ice bucket, along with two champagne flutes in front of a crackling fireplace. Light the candles, dim the room lights, and adjust the music to low.

On a table near the bed arrange in advance with room service for a delicious late-night snack. Keep in mind that it is very common for the bride and groom to be so busy at the reception that they miss much or all of their reception meal, so you'll want a light snack to be on hand. Perhaps a little smoked salmon, poached shrimp, and a dish of crisp-tender asparagus vinaigrette. For the ultimate in luxury, order an iced tin of caviar with a pair of mother-of-pearl spoons. For dessert, what could be sweeter than a bit of leftover wedding cake along with a few chocolate-dipped strawberries arranged on a silver tray? They're all sensual finger food–delicacies you can feed your bride, and vice versa.

Looking for even more romance? How about covering the bed and room with rose petals, so that the first thing your bride sees is a thick carpet of petals? When he has finished arranging the flowers for your reception, your florist can strew your hotel bedroom lavishly with rose petals for an extra touch of fantasy that makes an unforgettable memory. An alternative is to have the florist provide a basket of fragrant gardenia blooms that can be floated in the hot tub and placed around the room.

And last but not least, place a beautifully wrapped box containing a negligee on the bed and perhaps even a pair of matching slippers next to the bed. Not to be left out, you can peel off your wedding attire and ease into a pair of sexy silk boxers with a matching dressing gown, either bought by you or purchased by your bride as a gift. Uncork the champagne, pour two flutes full, and offer one to your new wife. I'll bet she'll raise it in a toast to you, a gentleman who understands the importance of romance. And remember, you have now set the standard for romance in the future.

Chapter 17

Making the Most of the Honeymoon

A beachfront bungalow in Fiji...a grand hotel in Venice...a horse ranch in Santa Barbara...a safari in Africa...whatever your taste in travel, your honeymoon can get your marriage off to the right start.

In the past the honeymoon destination was a secret known only to the groom, who would whisk his bride off to a spot that he alone had decided was ideal. I've always wondered: How did these hapless brides know what to pack?

Today the honeymoon is usually a joint expedition in every sense of the word. So before you call your travel agent, it makes sense to sit down with your fiancée and brainstorm your fantasy honeymoon. You don't have to let her know exactly what you have in mind; keep some surprises for later.

Answer these questions together as a starting point:

1. When you picture yourself in an idyllic spot, what is the setting? Is it on a mountaintop, by a beach, or on the winding streets of an Italian hill town?

2. Do you prefer tropical weather or more temperate climes?

3. Do you crave solitude, or do you like the excitement and fun of a city environment with lots of people around and sights to see?

4. What are your favorite pastimes—skiing, swimming, hiking, horseback riding, dining in fine restaurants?

5. When you vacation, do you like to do nothing at all, or do you prefer to be constantly on the run, visiting museums, dining in fine restaurants, and going to theater?

6. Are there certain things that are "musts" about a destination for you? For example, are gourmet restaurants an absolute necessity? Do you require creature comforts like an extra-large bed and modern bathrooms?

7. Is there a certain spot on earth you have always fantasized about visiting?

8. And last, you should consider your budget. Are you prepared to pay for five-star hotels, or is a funky little inn by the beach more your style?

Once you have each answered these questions, the right destination for your honeymoon should be easy to determine. If you want to do more research, the honeymoon sections of bridal magazines are a great place to start. There are incredible packages offered to honeymooners that can be ideal for couples on any budget. The Internet can also be a source of great ideas and contacts, although you should check them out carefully to be certain you are dealing with reputable firms. I highly recommend taking your requirements to a professional travel agent who specializes in vacation travel. He or she should be able to analyze your wish list, listen to your budget parameters, and come up with great recommendations.

If you like, you can still surprise your bride and keep your destination a secret by having her pick the kind of honeymoon location she wants, then letting you make the final arrangements. You can give her information on what to pack without revealing your destination.

I'm a believer in leaving on your honeymoon immediately after the wedding. Go away that same night, or the following day at the latest. Sometimes scheduling problems mean that a couple has to delay their honeymoon a week or so. You know what? That's too practical. The momentum and the fun are lost. Let the fairy tale of your wedding continue and get right on that plane, boat, or car.

The art of having a fabulous travel experience comes down to planning ahead. When you make your hotel reservation, tell them from the first phone call that you are on your honeymoon and be specific about any room requirements you have. Ascertain that you will have the room type you expect with the view that you want and that you will not be close to the elevator or above the kitchen. Of course, insist that all details be confirmed in writing, by mail or fax.

Once you have your reservation, ask to speak with the manager or concierge. Explain that you are on your honeymoon, and you want everything to be just right. Discuss your requirements, whether it be reservations at the best restaurants in town, theater tickets, passes to major museum shows, or any special room needs you may have. Ask about the weather at the time of year you will be visiting. Create a rapport with the manager over the telephone. If you have selected a top property, the hotelier will bend over backward to make sure you and your bride are enchanted with your stay. You may arrive to find a complimentary fruit basket and a bottle of bubbly chilling in an ice bucket along with a welcome note.

Planning ahead also means taking care of any paperwork needed for traveling to your destination. If a passport is needed, check whether yours and that of your bride must be renewed, and take care of this at least a month in advance of your honeymoon. Any required visas or other travel documents should also be obtained well ahead, either by mail or at the local consulate. Some off-the-beaten-track destinations require inoculations, so be sure to check with your travel agent.

Perhaps you are clever and have arranged to charge the major wedding-related expenses on your airline-affiliated credit card. Those miles–and they can add up with a wedding–may be enough to get you free upgrades or even free tickets. Traveling first or business class is a lovely way to pamper your bride on this first trip of your married life together. You'll both arrive more relaxed and refreshed without spending any additional money.

Also, check the fine print on your frequent-flyer membership information, because there may be various deals with car rental companies, hotels, or cruise ships that you can take advantage of.

Don't be done in by the details. All reservations should have confirmation numbers and be reconfirmed by phone well in advance of your departure.

On arrival, introduce yourself to your hotel contact, and discuss any last-minute requirements. I find that when one is straightforward and professional about one's expectations, the hotel staff generally responds in kind. If you are dissatisfied with your accommodations, let the staff know right away so that they can make every effort to correct the problem immediately.

Look for ways you can inject romance into your trip. Perhaps you want to spend one evening having a secluded room-service dinner for two under the stars on the patio of your hotel suite. The concierge can help you arrange everything, from the bottle of chardonnay in the ice bucket, to asking the singer from the hotel lounge to stand outside your patio and serenade your bride with her favorite romantic ballad.

What about giving your wife a romantic surprise every day of your honeymoon? Maybe the first morning it's breakfast in bed, the next day it's a little gift, the next it's an armful of flowers for the room, the next it's a box of chocolate truffles on her pillow, the following night it's hundreds of candles all over the room. It's a wonderful way of showing your thoughtfulness and love.

And don't forget the camera and film. You might not think it ever happens, but believe me, many couples wind up spending hours searching for a camera at their honeymoon destination rather than enjoying their trip!

The Traveling Gentleman

I fly constantly, and it always amazes me to see how carelessly people dress on planes. Out of courtesy to the other passengers, it's important to always look neat and well dressed while traveling, especially on your honeymoon. I always travel like I'm flying first class, especially if I'm not. Even if I'm dressing casually, my clothes are comfortable and neat. I bring a good-looking, practical carry-on bag that meets the airline size restrictions.(Check in advance by telephone, since the rules vary.) I know that if I run into an unforeseen problem on my trip and find myself at the mercy of some airline employee–and what frequent traveler hasn't experienced this?–I have a far better chance of receiving assistance than someone who looks like he just fell out of bed. When you look professional, you are treated professionally; it's as simple as that.

There's an art to the proper packing of luggage, and it separates the experienced man of the world from the neophyte traveler. Because I'm in and out of suitcases on a weekly if not daily basis and always have to look presentable when I arrive, I take packing seriously. I pack very lightly, taking clothes that work well together and travel well. I pack all my shirts in translucent flat plastic shirt bags, which are available from several mail-order catalogs. The shirts don't wrinkle the way they do if they're loose, and they're much easier to access, because every time I move a shirt from the suitcase to a drawer, I don't have to refold it. It makes packing and unpacking so much easier.

My shoes always travel with shoe trees and in shoe bags. This keeps the shoes from becoming

The Grateful Groom

As you dash off on your honeymoon, don't forget to thank the people who made your wedding a wonderful celebration. Pop some notecards in your carry-on bag, and take some time on the plane to express your gratitude to the important people, whether they be your best man, the caterer, the bandleader, or the officiant. Reserve your most heartfelt thanks for your parents and your in-laws, whether or not they were involved in the wedding. Remember that a well-written and sincere letter, sent promptly, means much more than a verbal thank-you or even a gift sent later. Express what you feel at this turning point in your life. Here's what one groom wrote to his parents:

Dear Mom and Dad,

Thank you so much for all of your assistance in making our wedding so wonderful and for being so accommodating with Jill's very large family. We are thoroughly enjoying the first few days of married life. On our nine-hour flight to Hawaii we spent at least eight and a half hours reliving every minute of the wedding.

I also want you to know how much I really appreciate all you've done for me to prepare me for this point in life. I've never felt more ready, and having you two as such a great example, I know what type of relationship I will be striving for in my life. Thank you for everything you've taught me and all the values you instilled in me. Please don't think you lost a son, but rather that you have gained a gorgeous daughter. We look forward to showing you our pictures when we return.

Love,

Jeff

crushed and prevents them from soiling my other clothing.

I have two sets of all my grooming essentials. One set I keep at home; the other always resides in my toiletry case, so that I can grab it at a moment's notice and hopefully not leave anything behind.

Finally, I never wait until the last minute to pack. That's how you forget critical items. I always tell brides and grooms who are preparing for their honeymoon that they should pack two days in advance. That way it's done; it's one less thing to worry about, and you won't arrive in Hawaii to find you forgot your brand-new, expensive swimsuit!

Honeymoon Check List

Airline Departure   Date and time: _____   Airline flight # _____

Airline Return   Date and time: _____   Airline flight # _____

Airline toll-free number: _____

Travel agent: _____

Telephone: _____   Facsimile: _____   E-mail: _____

Ground Transportation

Car rental company/Limousine company: _____

Telephone: _____   Facsimile: _____   E-mail: _____

Reservation/Pickup date/time: _____

Return date/time: _____

Confirmation # _____

Hotels

Name: _____

Telephone: _____   Facsimile: _____   E-mail: _____

Arrival date: _____   Departure date: _____

Confirmation # _____

Address: _____

Contact: _____

Special instructions: _____

Name: _____

Telephone: _____   Facsimile: _____   E-mail: _____

Arrival date: _____   Departure date: _____

Confirmation # _____

Address: _____

Contact: _____

Special instructions: _____

Special activities/Reservations: _____

Emergency contact information: _____

Passport numbers: _____   (his) _____   (hers) _____

Chapter 18

Dos and Don'ts of Getting Married

We have come a long way from the days when a couple planning a wedding had to worry constantly about breaking some esoteric etiquette rule. There are still a few levels of society where the traditional rules of etiquette are cast in bronze. But I find most people getting married today prefer a less traditional approach that paves the way for new, creative ideas and rituals.

Today's openness is a very positive thing, but weddings still aren't "anything goes" occasions. The same rules of social behavior and common courtesy apply today as they did in the past. The bride and groom must be careful to balance their desires and fantasies with common sense and consideration toward others in order to avoid conflicts and hurt feelings among family and friends.

Wedding traditions are now optional rather than the rule. But it's still important to be aware of traditions so that the bride and groom can decide whether those time-tested practices make sense in their situation. For example, the receiving line, once a wedding staple, is now often considered stilted and overly formal, in addition to the fact that it creates a huge unnecessary bottleneck. Some families, however, insist upon it as an assurance that the bride and groom and their immediate families have a chance to greet all the guests. Another change concerns engraved wedding invitations, which used to be almost mandatory. Now wedding invitations can be as creative as a couple wishes. Still, some couples who are planning a formal wedding send the traditional engraved invitation of black ink on white or ivory card stock, which telegraphs the formality of the occasion without a word.

My approach to weddings might be called "the new traditionalism," meaning the opportunity to create new rituals and new traditions. I like wedding traditions that make sense, such as the best man who takes on wedding-related assignments from the groom–but why should that be limited to the old-fashioned list of best-man duties? Maybe what the groom really needs is someone to entertain and charm the bride's mother on the morning of the wedding, so she won't have an anxiety attack. Who better than the best man!

Old Rules	New Trends
The man who wishes to ask a woman to marry him must first ask permission of her father.	When a couple wish to marry, the groom–and the bride, if she likes–should call on her parents and ask for their blessing.
When proposing, the suitor asks a woman to marry him while down on bended knee and	Proposals can be traditional or creative, but without an heirloom ring, I always recommend letting

proffering a diamond engagement ring.

The best man is responsible for a range of duties including helping the groom pack for the wedding and honeymoon, keeping the bride's wedding ring until the ceremony, giving the officiant his or her fee, handling transport of the bridal couple and their luggage after the reception, making a toast at the reception, and so on.

The bachelor party is an orgiastic bacchanal about which the less said, the better.

The bride's family pays for the wedding, while the groom's family hosts the rehearsal dinner.

No woman attending a wedding should wear white except the bride.

If a bride has been married before, she cannot wear white at her wedding.

Tuxedos are never worn before six P.M.

A cutaway ("morning coat") is appropriate for a daytime formal wedding.

The bride is escorted down the aisle by her father...her arm resting on his.

After the ceremony, the wedding party adjourns to the reception site, where a lengthy session of formal photography ensues.

the lady select the setting for her engagement ring.

A responsible best man who is willing to take on a myriad of wedding-related duties for the groom is worth his weight in gold. The duties need not be those traditionally assumed by best men but should instead be what needs to be done. Also, many of the best man's traditional duties are often assumed by a wedding consultant or party planner.

The bachelor party is an opportunity for a group of close friends to socialize and have fun in a civilized manner.

The bride, groom, and their families make sensible, fair decisions about who should assume which portion of the cost of the wedding.

White apparel is fine for non-brides, so long as they stay away from long, flowing white gowns!

The bride should wear what pleases her and suits the style of the wedding she has planned.

Tuxedos are never worn before six P.M.

A cutaway ("morning coat") is appropriate for a daytime formal wedding. But a good-looking suit may be a better option.

The bride may walk down the aisle with whomever she pleases, or unescorted if she prefers.

After the ceremony the wedding party adjourns to the reception site, where any formal photography follows a strict timetable so that the guests are not kept waiting longer than necessary and the wedding party can join the balance of the guests at the cocktail reception.

The wedding photographer takes a series of portrait photos of the bride, groom, their families, and the wedding party.

Today wedding photographers use a much more photojournalistic, documentary, candid style with fewer formal photos taken.

At the reception site the bride, groom, and wedding party form a receiving line to greet all the wedding guests.

I find the receiving line to be a completely outdated custom that creates a lengthy bottleneck between the ceremony and the cocktail reception and delays the wedding party from mingling informally with guests.

The tuxedo is traditionally worn with a black bow tie and black cummerbund.

Tuxedos may be updated by omitting the tie and cummerbund and wearing an elegant silk vest or perhaps a decorative button at the shirt collar.

The bride writes thank-you notes for each wedding gift received, making every attempt to send a note within one month of receiving the gift.

The bride and groom should share in the task of writing thank-you notes for the gifts they receive. Notes should be sent within a month of receiving each gift.

Rules, rules, rules.

Basically the only rule is that style should prevail in everything you do.

Chapter 19

Anniversaries—From Year One On

Let's put to rest the old cliché about the husband forgetting the wedding anniversary. In this day and age there really is no excuse. Software calendar programs, electronic organizers, notebook organizers—there are many simple ways to keep track of this once-a-year event.

So first of all program your anniversary in your personal calendar system as a "recurring event" for the rest of your life. If you're computerized, it will take just a few keystrokes. But entering that fateful date isn't enough. I think that twenty to thirty days ahead of the actual date, you should put in a pop-up reminder of the impending event so you can plan ahead and make reservations. Your anniversary should never sneak up on you—it's too important to your marriage. Celebrating your anniversary can also be a great way to put your relationship back on track if necessary and reassure your wife of your love and commitment.

Unfortunately, it is all too easy for couples to let their anniversary become rote. The husband brings home a corner-store bouquet and a last-minute bauble from Tiffany's. The wife gives him the putter he wanted. They go out to dinner. There's nothing wrong with that, except that too often it becomes automatic and therefore meaningless.

I feel that your anniversary should be an occasion to honor your marriage in a fun and creative way. You should focus on the things that will

Anniversary Traditions

There are long-standing traditions for anniversary gifts that some couples like to observe, but others choose to ignore. I consider them optional but offer them as possibilities.

1st	paper
2nd	cotton
3rd	leather
4th	linen, silk
5th	wood
6th	iron
7th	wool, copper, or brass
8th	bronze or electrical appliances
9th	pottery or china
10th	tin or aluminum
11th	steel
12th	silk, linen
13th	lace
14th	ivory or agate
15th	crystal or glass
20th	china
25th	silver
30th	pearls
40th	rubies or garnets
45th	sapphires or tourmalines
50th	gold
55th	emeralds or turquoise
60th	diamonds or gold
75th	diamonds or gold

A Thoughtful and Romantic Approach

A couple who are friends of mine trade responsibilities each year for the planning of their anniversary celebration, and they had a special anniversary coming up. Because it was the wife's turn, I worked with her to create an unforgettable weekend-long celebration for her husband.

On a Friday afternoon she met him at his office and surprised him by letting him know that a Town Car was waiting to whisk them away. She took him to the Hotel Bel-Air, where they checked into a lovely suite overlooking the hotel's Swan Lake. In the suite we had hung his favorite robe on a hook in the closet, placed his slippers beside the bed, put photos of the kids and several books by his favorite author on the nightstand, and filled a basket with his favorite snack foods. Soon after they were settled into the suite, a masseuse arrived, set up her table, and gave him an hour-long deep-tissue massage.

At just before eight P.M., there was a knock on the door, and a room-service waiter entered with a romantic dinner for two and a beautiful arrangement of cream-colored roses for the table, along with a sterling silver candelabra from their home. The menu was composed around the husband's favorite foods–caviar to start, followed by sautéed Dover sole, fresh asparagus, and a rich chocolate dessert. After dinner the happy couple retired to their private patio outside the suite, where fresh gardenia blossoms floated in the bubbling hot tub. On the ledge by the tub was a bottle of champagne in an ice bucket and a dish heaped with fresh strawberries and whipped cream.

The next morning after breakfast the wife led her husband out to the Bel-Air driveway, where he discovered she had rented his fantasy car for a day, a white convertible Rolls-Royce. Off they went to the country club to play nine holes of golf. Then a quick lunch in Beverly Hills and a round of shopping at his favorite stores. Late in the after-

make your wife happy. Does she long to have a "day of beauty" at a local day spa? Has she talked about taking French lessons or a cooking course? Does she love to shop for clothes? Your objective should be to make her wish come true on your anniversary. Or if you really want to spoil her, do all of the above, followed by a romantic dinner and a night in the honeymoon suite of your favorite hotel.

Of course, the anniversary isn't just about a gift. It's a ritual. Perhaps both of you agree that your lives are full enough and gifts aren't necessary. You should still celebrate your anniversary in a way that will show your commitment and love to your spouse. It could be as simple as sending the kids to your parents' house for the weekend so you can focus on each other for forty-eight hours, or it could be that you hire a local chef to come to your home and cook a romantic meal for two and use all the silver and crystal you registered for when getting married. It could be a getaway weekend at an inn on the beach or a great resort hotel with spa facilities.

The important thing is that no matter how you celebrate, take the time to tell your wife how much the past year has meant to you and how happy you are to be spending your life with her. Write it down in a love letter, if you like, and place it on her pillow. Some wives wait all their lives to hear or read such loving words from their spouses. Give your wife the gift of your tender, loving communication, and the gift will come back to you tenfold, I assure you. A well-written love note is worth much more than a last-minute gift.

Major anniversaries–the fifth, the tenth–require

more thought and planning. Such occasions might call for an engraved piece of jewelry or a trip to a destination she has always wanted to visit, or perhaps a party with all your family and friends–important gifts and celebrations for an important occasion.

Speaking of anniversaries, here's a little hint. I always used to find myself making special trips at the last minute to search for birthday and anniversary cards–until I got smart. Now I buy them in advance, in quantity. I go to my favorite card store and select a variety of cards with specific people in mind, fifteen or twenty at a time. Now I almost always have the right card for the right occasion.

noon they took a scenic drive up the Pacific Coast Highway past Malibu, then drove back on Sunset Boulevard to the hotel.

Plans were for them to attend a previously scheduled dinner party, but on the way she suggested they stop at a friend's house for a drink. There, to her husband's delight, was a surprise party of ten of their best friends. They had a wonderful evening. But the night was not yet over; back at the hotel the husband walked into the suite to find the lights turned low, romantic music playing, the bed covered with rose petals, and a hundred votive candles flickering.

The next day the couple checked out of the hotel to go for a hike in Will Rogers State Park. After an invigorating two-hour hike, they arrived at a clearing to find their nanny with their two children and a delicious picnic laid out for their enjoyment. They spent the afternoon exploring the park with the kids.

When they finally returned home, the husband told his wife that, in his wildest fantasies, he could never have come up with a better anniversary celebration. It's my opinion that what made this anniversary so special was not the money spent, which was considerable, but the care the wife took to focus on things her husband really loved.

Here are some traditional anniversary gifts–and great alternatives.

Traditional	Nontraditional
Eternity ring	Cooking class in France
Gold watch	Season tickets to the opera
Jewelry box	Tennis lessons
Diamond tennis bracelet	Year pass to day spa
Weekend at a resort	Donation to favorite charity
Piece of jewelry	Well-written love note

Chapter 20

The Honeymoon Is Over

The early months of your marriage are when you begin to create your own style as a couple. You can develop a style that is an extension of your personalities and will last throughout your married life, or you can drift along without any sense of direction or plan. As newlyweds, you may be utterly wrapped up in each other, but don't lose track of your friends and the people who are important in your lives. When a couple marries, it's all too easy to drift apart from old friends. But it doesn't have to happen. Maintaining good relationships with the people who are important to you takes effort. You have to pick up the phone and call. You have to make firm plans to get together. When you do, it will enrich your lives with wonderful experiences. But you have to make the first move and not wait for others to call you to stay in touch.

Keep in mind that every time you interface with someone, you are building your image as a couple. You need to decide with your fiancée: Are you going to be Mr. and Mrs. Always Late, Mr. and Mrs. Never RSVP, Mr. and Mrs. Don't Write Thank-You Notes, Mr. and Mrs. Can't Get It Together? Wouldn't you rather be Mr. and Mrs. Happening?

The Art of the Thank-You Note

The simple fact is that by incorporating graciousness and consideration into your dealings with others, you will make the appropriate impression. Hopefully you have gotten off on the right foot by diligently writing thank-you notes for all the wonderful wedding presents you received from your friends and relations. Continuing this practice throughout your married life will solidify your reputation as a couple who goes out of their way to show their gratitude. And thank-you notes are not just for your bride to write, either. You should be expressing your thanks in writing routinely to anyone who gives you presents, entertains you at dinner, refers business to you, or does you a favor.

A proper thank-you note takes almost no time at all. I write them constantly and have developed a style that is easy and natural. First, if you recently spent time with the person, refer to that meeting and the pleasure you took from it. Then thank the person for the gift, service, or favor, mentioning how useful it will be, how beautiful it is, how much you appreciate it–whatever's appropriate. Just say what you mean. If you express yourself naturally, the note will almost write itself. A thank-you note doesn't have to be pages long, but it should be specific, gracious, and sincere.

Don't tell me you don't have time for thank-you notes. You don't have time not to write them. Failing to write thank-you notes is rude and ungrateful. It will hurt you in the long run. And once you get the knack of it, writing a thank-you note takes, literally, about sixty seconds.

Here's an example:

Dear John,

It was wonderful seeing you at lunch the other day. I certainly enjoyed the crab claws. It's a pity they're not served year round. Thank you very much for introducing me to Richard from Fidelity. It looks like we will do business together. I hope to see you again soon. Please stay in touch.

Sincerely,

Ralph

Dear Lisa,

I so much enjoyed the evening we spent together and the chance to meet your husband. The visit to your home made my business trip almost bearable. Dinner was delicious. I'm still thinking about that chocolate dessert. Remember you promised to fax me the recipe. Karen sends her love. When are you coming to the West Coast?

Best,

Charles

A final word on thank-you notes. I run a very busy business, and I'm always on the road traveling. Whether I'm at home or traveling, I find that people are constantly entertaining me and sending me beautiful flowers and gifts, for which I'm very grateful. I travel with a transparent plastic folio containing about twenty sheets of my personal letterhead, twenty envelopes, and lots of stamps. I write thank-you notes on the plane or when I get to my hotel room while waiting for my next engagement. Then I give them to the front desk to mail. It couldn't be easier. People are always so appreciative when they receive a prompt, handwritten thank-you note.

Thoughtful Gift-Giving

Knowing when to send a gift and what to send is an art. I think it is very gracious to send a gift on special occasions, or when you want to express gratitude but feel a thank-you note may be inadequate. A gift doesn't have to be expensive, but it should be of very good quality.

When you have been invited to someone's home for an overnight stay, a meal, or even cocktails, a small, well-chosen gift tells the host you appreciate the hospitality. Never arrive empty-handed at someone's home–unless, of course, you have sent over flowers, chocolates, or wine earlier in the day or plan to send something the next day. If you are invited for a meal, I always recommend having flowers sent directly from the florist earlier on the day of the event, or the day after along with a thank-you note, instead of bringing them with you. When you arrive with an armful of flowers, it may make you look like Lord Bountiful, but it forces your hostess to drop what she is doing, put on her floral designer hat, and spend several minutes hunting down a vase and arranging the blooms, which distracts her from being a hostess.

Because none of us has much time for shopping, it's a good idea to have a repertoire of gifts that you know your friends and acquaintances will like. I have several "staple" gifts that I keep on hand in quantity for when I need them. Since everyone's taste is different, you should develop your own collection of gifts so that you won't have to hunt all over town the next time you need a little something. Of course, such a well-chosen gift should be attractively wrapped, tied with a ribbon, and accompanied by a thoughtfully worded card.

My secret tactic that ensures I always have a house gift is to stock a case of champagne, a case of wine, and a dozen boxed fragrant candles in my coat closet near the door. Each bottle and candle is individually gift wrapped, tied with a ribbon imprinted "Best wishes from Colin" (I order inexpensive personalized ribbon from a gift catalog), and placed in a gift bag. With a cache of gifts at hand, I can quickly grab one as I'm heading out the door, so I never arrive empty-handed.

Here are some ideas for great gifts:

- Scented candle in an attractive box
- Inlaid wood picture frame
- Box of fine imported chocolates or chocolate truffles
- Leather-bound photo album
- Fountain or ball pen
- A book–the sort of volume that people seldom buy for themselves but that they always love, on a subject such as gardening, antiques, coffee, home decor, cigars
- Gorgeous floral arrangement
- Bottle of champagne
- Bottle of fine wine
- Bottle of fine liquor, such as cognac, small-batch bourbon, or single-malt scotch
- Basket of exotic fresh fruit, such as blood oranges, starfruit, cheremoyas, or miniature pears
- Herb garden in a terra-cotta pot

Special Occasions

One of the most thoughtful things you can do for friends and relatives is remember their birthdays, anniversaries, and special days. A humorous greeting card on a friend's birthday, a supportive note to a widower on the anniversary of his wife's death–these are the gestures that show others how much we think and care about them.

The best way to make sure you keep track of these important days is to have one of you–preferably whomever is more organized–enter them on his or her calendar program as annual events. Most of these programs have little pop-up alarms that you can set for a week ahead of time, alerting you to send a card or perhaps a little gift. It's a thoughtful way of staying in touch with the people who are important to you.

The Favor of a Reply Is Requested

There's an art to being a good guest, just as there is to being a skilled host. A thoughtful guest always responds promptly to invitations. *RSVP* means *"répondez, s'il vous plaît,"* or as some have quipped, "reserved seating varnished and polished." In other words, please reply. It does not mean respond only if you are coming, or respond the morning of the event. It means check your calendar, decide with your wife if you are available to attend, put the engagement on your calendar, and make that phone call or return the response card. I am continually amazed by the number of people who fail to respond to invitations, forcing the host or hostess to get on the phone and beg for an answer.

My other personal pet peeve is guests who do accept an invitation but then call hours before the event or even at the last minute and cancel. This seems to be the era when people believe that if they don't happen to feel like doing something at the moment, they don't have to. They never consider that the person who invited them may have gone to a great deal of trouble on their account. When you accept an engagement, unless you have a medical emergency or a death in the family, you should show up. Commitments you make to others are important and deserve to be honored, just as you want your invitations to be honored when you issue them.

Punctuality

One of the most considerate things you can do when you are invited to someone's home, or to a restaurant, or to any meeting, is arrive on time. There's no such thing as being "fashionably late"! Fashionably late, to me, means unfashionably disrespectful.

Regrettably we have so lost touch with the concept of punctuality that I see guests wandering into dinner parties an hour or an hour and a half after the invitation time, often without an apology or even a good reason for their tardiness. I find this shocking. It is terribly rude not only to the host but to the other guests, who may be kept waiting while dinner is delayed. Certainly, we all experience an unexpected crisis, traffic jam, or other event that may delay us a few times a year. But if it happens routinely, you should address your punctuality problem by leaving earlier. Otherwise you may get a reputation as the couple who just doesn't care about others.

It often happens with couples that one person is chronically late, while the other is punctual. It is up to the punctual one to see that as a couple, you treat others considerately and arrive at the appointed hour. This sometimes means you have to play little tricks, like telling your mate the dinner party is set for seven P.M., when you actually were invited for seven-thirty. I'm in favor of this sort of minor stretching of the truth if it gets you where you need to be on time.

And just think about the benefits when you do arrive on time. Your host or hostess probably has fewer guests to focus on, so you'll receive lots of attention. You'll get the freshest drinks, first crack at the canapés, and the best seats in the living room!

Entertaining in Your Home

I am sure you will agree that some of our most memorable moments are those spent around the dinner table. One of life's great pleasures is inviting friends into our home to share quality time with them–in other words, entertaining. Your engagement and the early months of your marriage are an ideal opportunity to begin to develop your entertaining style as a couple. Entertaining can be a shared pleasure, one you can do together throughout your marriage, adjusting your style as you please.

When deciding how you want to entertain, look at each of your talents and decide how much time you realistically have to put into this. Perhaps you, the groom, are the talented chef and want to take charge of the cooking or choosing the wine. In that case maybe your bride can handle buying and arranging the flowers, setting up the bar, setting the table, and/or doing the dishes. Play off your strengths and hers. Maybe you love grilling on the top-of-the-line barbecue that you received as a wedding gift. Assemble your guests outdoors with some wine and cheese and let them chat while you grill their dinner. Or perhaps you have a great wine cellar and take pleasure in serving a different wine with each course. Maybe you are an expert bartender and want to showcase your talents at cocktail parties rather than dinners. With one couple I know, the man, a busy cardiac surgeon, has no interest in cooking dinner but absolutely loves to mix spirited cocktails and concoct elaborate desserts. Dinner at this couple's home is a much-anticipated occasion because his desserts are like those served at top-tier restaurants. Often I'll call them, invite them to my home for dinner, and ask them to bring a dessert. It makes for a great evening.

What if you feel your cooking skills are inadequate and you'd like to improve? Or perhaps you don't know much about wine but would like to serve nice bottles to your friends. It's just a matter of starting small and spending time along the way trying to learn new things. Take a cooking class with your wife; practice making several recipes just for the two of you, or have a chef come and cook for you and a small group of friends. Once you have a few delicious dishes in your repertoire, then you can begin to have small lunches or dinner parties, just one or two couples to start. Keep it simple and easy until your confidence grows.

It's the same with wine. You can take a wine class, but I think the best way to learn about wine is to actually taste it and read about what you're tasting. Many wine stores have a regular program of wine tastings and wine dinners, where wines are paired with each course. Wine magazines are another good source of ideas on wines to serve at home. If you need guidance on wines to go with a specific

My Secrets to Being a Great Host

I always keep a few bottles of good champagne and white wine chilled in the refrigerator and one or two bottles of vodka in the freezer. Life offers us many occasions for celebration and a glass of chilled bubbly or tasty cocktail makes any celebration more festive. (A glass of chilled bubbly is wonderful for no special occasion at all. And it can be just the thing to chase the blues away.)

The cocktail hour is just that: an hour. Dinner should be served within an hour after the first guests have arrived. If a few people arrive late, that's no reason to delay dinner and punish the guests who arrived on time. Remove the place settings of those who haven't arrived, and start the dinner on time.

When seating guests, cluster people together for more intimacy and energy. If you have a large table and a small group, place the people at one end. If you space guests widely apart at a long table, you might as well be e-mailing one another. Try to seat guests boy-girl-boy-girl, and separate couples to encourage conversation.

Serve hot food hot and cold food cold.

Don't serve huge portions, but have second helpings available for guests who are still hungry.

Serve plenty of water with dinner. It's good for the digestion and makes it less likely that guests will drink too much.

White wine should be well chilled. It's much easier to let the wine warm up at the table if it's too cold than chill it down once it's been poured. Red wine should be served at cool room temperature and can even be chilled for a half hour if the weather is hot.

Don't overfill the wineglasses. It is important to leave enough room in the glass for guests to swirl the wine and appreciate its bouquet. Four to six ounces of wine is a good-sized pour, depending on the size of your glasses.

menu, find a well-informed staffer at a good wine store, and fax him or her your menu and price range. The staffer should be able to make several recommendations that will please you and your guests. Tasting new and unfamiliar wines with food is a great way to begin to learn about what you like and don't like, and why.

Perhaps neither of you likes to cook. Not cooking should never be a rationale for not entertaining! Simply compose a menu of wonderful take-out items, or dishes from your favorite local restaurant, and serve them. People will love it.

The main thing to remember about entertaining is that it requires some planning, which can be part of the fun. A few days to a week before the event, take the time to sit down and think about what you would like to do for your guests. Are we going to do it indoors or outdoors? Will it be casual, or will we call a florist to help with the table? What do we want to serve? Once you have decided on the ambience, you need a game plan as to who will buy the wine and the food, who's going to compose the menu, who's going to do the cooking, who's going to pick up around the house beforehand, and who's going to clean up afterward.

I have always said that inviting friends into your home for a meal needn't require days in the kitchen. You get no medals for doing everything from scratch. Most of us are busy, working people, or have the responsibilities of kids, and don't want to be chained to a stove for endless hours. Take advantage of the best food resources that are available to you—restaurants, gourmet take-out stores, delis, bakeries, and caterers—serve the food beautifully on your china, and no one will complain. A joint expedition to a gourmet deli can even be fun, as you discuss the various options, decide what you want to serve, and make your selections, maybe even discovering some cheeses you're not familiar with or a new ethnic food item you would like to try.

There's also no rule that says you have to entertain on an elaborate scale. If you prefer casual get-togethers, buy some delicious crusty bread, whip up a pot of chili and a salad, uncork a couple of bottles of California zinfandel, and you have the makings for a terrific informal evening with friends. Or invite friends for Saturday or Sunday brunch. You have the luxury of time, and hopefully no one has a tight schedule so people can relax. You don't have to be a rocket scientist to make pancakes or scramble some eggs, cook some bacon, and brew a great pot of strong coffee.

If you're going out to a show or to a restaurant for dinner with a group of friends, ask them back to your home for dessert. This is a nearly effortless way to entertain. Simply offer a couple of delicious desserts–homemade or purchased from a good pastry shop or bakery–along with a modest selection of after-dinner drinks and decaf coffee. A couple of cigars for the guys is a great way to complete the evening.

Another wonderful idea is the potluck supper. Invite a group of six or eight couples, and ask each to be responsible for one aspect of the dinner: an appetizer, a main course, side dish, dessert, wine, and so on. With very little effort, you can put together a lovely dinner party and

What do you do when one of your guests calls at the last minute and asks if he or she can bring her child or children? Tell the guest, "Sure, you can bring your kids. Have them bring their favorite video, and I'll order a pizza, and we'll seat them in the den." You're not saying no, but you're also letting the guest know that this is an adult party.

I prefer not to have smoking between courses or before the dessert dishes have been cleared away. I'm not wild about smoking at the table anyway, unless it's after the meal has been served and no one at the table objects. If guests choose to smoke cigars, I recommend moving to a well-ventilated room or outdoors on the patio if possible. If you have guests who enjoy cigars and some who don't, accommodate both by arranging for a private area for smoking after dinner, indoors or out.

When each course is finished, clear the table but never start doing the dishes while the guests are still present. It's terrible for one of the hosts to be away from the guests for a long period. If you start doing the dishes, it puts a real damper on the party and makes guests feel as though they've overstayed their welcome or, worse, that they should pitch in and help.

Stocking the Bar

A gracious host always keeps a well-stocked bar so that he can whip up a cooling libation at a moment's notice. Following is a list of the basic items the home bar should have. If you serve drinks often, you will want to augment this with other wine, spirits, or ingredients to make your specialties.

Equipment

Bottle opener

Champagne stopper

Citrus reamer

Corkscrew

Cocktail shaker with strainer

Ice bucket and ice tongs

Paring knife

Pitcher for water

Shot glass, jigger, or other measuring cup

Glassware

Old-fashioned glasses

Highball glasses

Martini glasses

Wineglasses

Water glasses

Champagne flutes

Brandy snifters*

Pilsner glasses*

*optional

Wine and Liquor

Blended whiskey

Brandy

Bourbon

Cognac

enjoy time with your friends and not in the kitchen. (Just make sure that, if you have a friend who is notoriously late, you assign him or her the dessert, not the appetizers.)

I love the idea of collaborative entertaining—inviting friends to bring something and composing a wonderful party out of it. You can do this in so many ways:

• Have a caviar tasting, with each couple bringing two ounces of caviar and a bottle of champagne or frozen vodka. The host can supply toast points and other caviar accompaniments.

• Ask each guest to bring a bottle of California zinfandel and an appetizer, main course, or dessert (chocolate can be delicious with some zinfandels) to go with it. Taste the wines without food first, then move on to the meal. I always look around the table halfway through the meal to see which bottle has been emptied first—it's a sure sign of the best wine with the food.

• In warm weather have each couple bring a food item that can be cooked on your barbecue grill. Guests can dine all evening on an eclectic menu of freshly grilled veggies, meats, poultry, and fish. Finish the dinner with a rich dessert (homemade or store-bought) like devil's food cake, strawberry shortcake, or ice cream.

However you decide to entertain, plan in advance. Decide with your bride who is responsible for what, and work out a schedule. You may want to make up a checklist of the things that need to be done by each of you. Remember, the most important consideration is to spend quality time with your guests, not to sequester yourself (or your bride) in the kitchen working on the food or doing the dishes. Do as much in advance as possible to leave time for your guests.

Since first impressions are so important, be sure to set the stage for a great party. When your guests arrive, the house should be tidy, the bar set up, the lights turned low, the candles lit, and the music playing. You should greet your guests heartily, and never make them wait for a drink, either; pretend they're coming in parched from the desert, and put a drink in their hands immediately. Good cocktails break the ice and instantly make your guests feel welcome. Instead of serving the standard red or white wine, mix a pitcher of margaritas, martinis, cosmopolitans, or any other great cocktail. You'll be amazed how quickly it jump-starts your party.

Because you and your wife are the center of energy at your parties, you should never leave your guests alone. When one of you needs to fix drinks or attend to something in the kitchen, be sure the other remains to chat with the guests. If one of you is answering the door, the other should be attending to the guests who have already arrived.

If guests arrive who do not know the others, it is your responsibility to introduce them to those who are already there and, if possible, start a conversation by remarking on a shared interest. "Dennis, this is Louis Mendez, a very good friend of mine. Louis, this is Dennis Hanrahan, who I know I've mentioned to you because he is my secret source for Knicks tickets." Immediately Louis, who loves the Knicks, has something to discuss with Dennis. If this conversational technique doesn't come naturally to you, practice it! It's a

Gin

Rum

Scotch—one blended, one single malt

Vodka

Tequila

White (dry) and red (sweet) vermouth

White and red table wine of good quality (chardonnay or sauvignon blanc for the white and a Chianti classico, pinot noir, or zinfandel for the red)

Specialty Liquors, Liqueurs, and Wines

Campari

Cherry brandy

Cointreau orange liqueur

Crème de cassis (if you serve kirs)

Crème de cacao

Pernod or Ricard

Sake

Sambuca

Sherry, dry

Mixers

Club soda

Soft drinks

Tonic water

Flavorings and Garnishes

Angostura bitters

Lemons

Limes

Maraschino cherries

Green olives

Sugar syrup or superfine sugar

Tabasco sauce

Worcestershire sauce

Cocktails

Brandy Alexander

Perfect when guests gather at your home after the theater.

1-1/2 ounces brandy

1 ounce dark crème de cacao

1 ounce half-and-half

1/4 teaspoon grated nutmeg

Combine brandy, crème de cacao, and half-and-half in a cocktail shaker half-filled with ice; shake well. Strain into a stemmed glass, and sprinkle nutmeg on top.

Champagne Cocktail

To get the evening off to a sparkling start.

1 sugar cube

1 generous dash Angostura bitters

6 ounces chilled dry champagne or champagne-method sparkling wine

Twist of lemon peel

Place the sugar cube in a stemmed glass, and saturate it with bitters. Top up with champagne, rub lemon peel along the rim of the glass, and drop it in.

Cosmopolitan

A recent innovation, this is one of the most popular cocktails at today's hottest bars.

2 ounces lemon-flavored vodka

1 ounce Cointreau orange liqueur

1/4 ounce lime juice

1 ounce cranberry juice

Combine all ingredients with ice in a cocktail shaker; shake until ice-cold. Strain into a prechilled martini glass.

good idea to spend a few minutes before any get-together thinking about interests your guests have in common so that the conversation will flow easily. It's the sort of thing that can make the difference between a dull party and a great one.

When introducing people, don't give titles or refer to someone's position in the corporate hierarchy. We are entertaining not to impress people but to share quality time with them.

As the guests are chatting, it's your job as host to make sure that everyone is drawn into the conversation, no one feels left out, and no one dominates the conversation to the exclusion of others. If a guest is sitting on the conversational sidelines, ask a question to draw him or her out. If someone is behaving like a big mouth, jump in and change the subject. You are the arbiter of the conversation at your parties, and your role is to control the energy so that everyone has a good time and feels included.

Occasionally you may have to resort to conversational games. I gave a dinner a while ago where a lot of the guests were my business acquaintances who didn't know each other. When the conversation lagged at the table, I took over and suggested that we go around the room and each tell our most embarrassing story. I got the ball rolling with the story of how I once accidentally locked myself out of my hotel room. I had called room service and asked them to collect my breakfast tray. Rather than have them come into the room, I wanted to place the tray outside the door. I was setting the tray down away from the door in the hallway when all of a sudden the door slammed shut, and I was left standing stark naked in the hall, with only a napkin between me and indecency! By the time we got around to the third person's tale of woe, the guests were shrieking with laughter. The ice was broken; the party took on a whole new energy, and everyone had a fabulous evening.

Entertaining in a Restaurant

Many couples find they are entertaining at restaurants more and more frequently. Sometimes these are business gatherings, but restaurant entertaining can be a wonderful way to host a group of friends if you are unable to invite them to your home.

There's an art to restaurant entertaining, and it's not as effortless as it looks. Again, advance planning is the key to making it look easy. First, ascertain if the restaurant has a staff person who is responsible for dealing with private parties, and make sure this is the person with whom you make all the arrangements. Contact the establishment well in advance and book the space for your group, whether it be a table or a private room. If the group is larger than eight, a secluded area of the restaurant or a private room works far better than being seated in the main dining area. Make sure your contact at the restaurant understands the importance of your event and that you expect your reservation to be honored with guests shown to the table immediately.

I recommend arranging the seating in advance. That way you can be sure that couples are separated and balance the energy at the table. I often messenger a set of place cards along with a seating plan to my contact at the restaurant so

Daiquiri

The most delicious daiquiris are made with fine aged or *añejo* rum.

1-1/2 ounces rum

1 ounce sugar syrup (or more to taste)

1 ounce freshly squeezed lime juice

Shake ingredients in a cocktail shaker half-filled with ice; strain and serve straight up or on the rocks.

Madras

Curiously refreshing.

1-1/2 ounces vodka

2 ounces cranberry juice

2 ounces orange juice

Pour ingredients over ice in a highball glass; stir.

Manhattan

A thoroughly civilized drink that reportedly was developed at the Manhattan Club in New York for Lady Jenny Churchill, Sir Winston's mother, according to Gary Regan's *The Bartender's Bible* (HarperCollins, 1991).

2 ounces blended whiskey

3/4 ounce sweet vermouth

Generous dash of Angostura bitters

Maraschino cherry

Stir whiskey, vermouth, and bitters with ice in a cocktail pitcher, and strain into a stemmed martini glass. Garnish with maraschino cherry.

Margarita

The better the tequila, the smoother the drink.

Coarse salt in a saucer

2 ounces 100 percent agave tequila

1/2 ounce Cointreau orange liqueur

1/2 ounce sugar syrup

2 ounces freshly squeezed lime juice, plus a few drops for moistening rim of glass

Moisten the rim of a cocktail glass with lime juice, and carefully dip it into salt, shaking off excess. Set aside. Combine remaining ingredients in a shaker half-filled with ice, and shake. Strain into cocktail glass, and serve straight up or on the rocks.

Martini

The classic, which has spawned dozens of variations.

2 ounces fine imported gin or vodka

1/2 to 1 ounce French (dry) vermouth

1 rinsed green olive

Stir gin or vodka and vermouth with ice in a pitcher. When ice-cold, strain into a prechilled martini glass, and garnish with olive.

Mojito

This Cuban rum drink will most certainly get your next party going.

1 tablespoon sugar syrup (see below)

4–5 fresh mint leaves

1-1/2 ounces dark rum

Juice of 1 fresh lime

Crushed ice

In an old-fashioned glass, use a wooden spoon to muddle (crush) mint leaves with sugar syrup. Add rum and lime juice. Fill with crushed ice and stir.

that everything will be ready when I arrive. For special celebrations a floral centerpiece makes the event even more personal.

If you have a large group, it is a good idea to plan the menu with the restaurant in advance, or at least plan the first courses and dessert, perhaps offering the guests a choice of entrée. This will help the restaurant serve the meal more efficiently, and it will also assist you in maintaining control over the cost. You should also select the champagne or wine ahead of time. When the guests arrive, white wine or champagne should be waiting by the table in an ice bucket, while a red may be opened and left to breathe on the table.

Always arrange to prepay with a 20 percent gratuity. That way there's no awkwardness at the end of the meal with people offering to pay their share. It's much more gracious to be able to say, "It's all been taken care of."

Finally, confirm every detail of your arrangements for your dinner in writing, via fax, to avoid any misunderstanding about your expectations.

Entertaining in a Hotel Suite

The fact that you are traveling does not mean you are at the mercy of restaurants when you would like to host friends or business contacts for drinks or dinner. Entertaining can be done very graciously in a hotel suite, although naturally it can be expensive. I recommend entertaining only in a suite that has a living room. Under no circumstances would you entertain anyone (besides your fiancée, of course!) in a standard hotel room where the bed is visible.

The fact that you may be staying in a full-service hotel doesn't relieve you of all responsibility for catering to your guests. This kind of entertaining requires a bit of advance planning, or you can leave an inhospitable impression. I remember the time when an associate and I were invited for drinks by an acquaintance of ours who was staying in a well-appointed suite in Manhattan. When we walked in, she was on the phone. "Help yourself," she said, covering the receiver and gesturing vaguely at the television set. It took a second for me to realize that we were meant to help ourselves to drinks from her minibar while she concluded her phone call. There was no ice evident. I had been looking forward to a scotch on the rocks but settled for a soft drink. Our "hostess" made us feel awkward because she had not bothered to arrange the makings for drinks beforehand, even with all the services of the hotel available to her. (Of course, it was also rude not to put aside her phone call while she greeted us.) When it came time for dinner, we were handed a room-service menu. We were left with a feeling that this young woman hadn't a clue how to deal with people in a gracious manner—not a great first impression for anyone to give.

I have on many occasions entertained in hotel suites and had very successful dinners. It takes just a bit of planning ahead. Well before your guests arrive, speak with the room-service manager, and order an adequate supply of ice, glasses, lemons or limes, a small knife, cocktail napkins, and any other ingredients you think you may need. You may order in wine or liquor from room-service, bring bottles in yourself, or

Negroni

An acquired taste, but once acquired, some people find these addictive.

1 ounce Campari

1 ounce gin

1 ounce sweet vermouth

Twist of lemon peel

Shake Campari, gin, and vermouth with ice in a cocktail shaker; strain into a martini glass. Run lemon peel around the rim of the glass, and drop it in.

Old-Fashioned

A delicious drink that tastes particularly good during the winter months.

1/2 teaspoon granulated sugar

2 dashes Angostura bitters

2 ounces bourbon whiskey

Orange slice

Maraschino cherry

Club soda

In an old-fashioned glass muddle sugar with bitters until sugar melts. Add bourbon and a generous handful of ice. Top with desired amount of club soda—one to two ounces. Garnish with orange slice and cherry, adding a spoonful of maraschino cherry liquid if desired.

Screwdriver

A wonderful drink for Sunday brunch.

2 ounces vodka

6 ounces freshly squeezed orange juice

Combine ingredients over ice in a highball glass.

Side Car

Another classic drink that's enjoying a renaissance. I make my side cars with slightly different proportions than the classic recipe.

1-1/2 ounces brandy

3/4 ounce Cointreau orange liqueur

1 ounce freshly squeezed lemon juice

Shake with ice, and strain into a martini glass; serve.

Sea Breeze

A Sunday afternoon by the beach and a sea breeze–what could be better?

1-1/2 ounces vodka

2 ounces grapefruit juice

3 ounces cranberry juice

Lime wedge

Combine vodka and juices over ice in a highball glass; garnish with lime wedge.

Singapore Sling

There are many versions of this classic drink, the original of which was created at the Raffles Hotel in Singapore. This is my favorite.

1 ounce gin

1 teaspoon sugar syrup

1 ounce lemon juice

1 ounce cherry brandy

Club soda

Shake first four ingredients with ice in a shaker; strain over ice into a highball glass. Add two to three ounces club soda to taste; stir.

use the minibar, although the latter will seldom be adequate for more than one round of drinks. The menu for dinner can also be arranged in advance. In a well-staffed hotel you can treat your guests as personally as if you were entertaining at home.

Hosting Overnight Guests in Your Home

When you had a bachelor pad, you could get away with sticking a buddy on the sofa when he stayed overnight. Now that you're married, the standards are a bit different! You don't have to make guests feel like they're staying at the Ritz, but the accommodations should certainly look like you've taken some time and effort to prepare for your guest.

A dedicated guest bedroom or den with a soft bed makes hosting overnight guests easier. But a lot of us don't have that much space and must temporarily convert a den or spare room into a guest room. A few touches will show guests your concern for their comfort and your pleasure in having them stay. First, make space in a closet for your guest's hanging clothes and in a chest of drawers for their folded things. The bed should be made with fresh sheets, of course, and fresh towels should be hung in their bathroom or placed on their bed. There should be some way to control the temperature, whether by opening a window or by using the thermostat for heating or air conditioning; if it's cool, an extra blanket should be folded at the foot of the bed. Check that there is good light for reading next to the head of the bed. A bottle or carafe of mineral water on the nightstand, along with a little bouquet of fresh flowers or a basket of fruit with a plate, napkin, and knife, are thoughtful additions. I always add a fragrant candle, a couple of recent paperback books, and a little preprinted card that has a few helpful suggestions for my guests, such as which phone line to use and where the keys are placed. Remember to always provide your own phone number, fax number, and address to guests, who may need this information when arranging taxi pickup or staying in touch with their offices.

Finally, when you settle the guests into their room, always ask if there is anything they need or anything you can do to make them more comfortable. Frequently people need a little prompting to express their needs, and your guests will appreciate your extra effort.

Sugar Syrup for Cocktails

2 cups granulated sugar

1 cup water

Mix ingredients in a saucepan, and bring to a boil, stirring. Simmer for five minutes, stirring occasionally, until sugar is dissolved. Let cool, pour into clean bottle, and store in refrigerator.

Note: If you are too impatient to make a simple syrup, two teaspoons superfine sugar can be stirred into an ounce of water until dissolved and substituted for the syrup. Just don't try adding sugar to a cocktail; sugar doesn't dissolve in alcohol.

A Word to the Groom

Your engagement is a wonderful time of transition and preparation for a major life change: marriage. I hope that you will take the advice in this book to heart and put into practice the techniques and guidelines that seem right for you. Whether it's deciding that you want to behave in a more gentlemanly fashion, or that you should put more of your personal stamp on the design and planning of your wedding, the steps you take now will not only help you enjoy your wedding more, they will enhance your relationships with your fiancée, your families, your friends, and your business acquaintances.

There's no better time than now to put this advice into practice. After your wedding you embark on a new life with your bride. It's one of those unique times in life when you can decide how you want to be perceived as a man, and as a couple, and make the changes necessary to achieve your goals.

The techniques and guidelines outlined in this book have served me well my entire life and have always stood me in good stead in a variety of circumstances: meeting new clients, helping a friend through a difficult time, or entertaining family and friends in my home. Behaving like a gentleman and knowing how to treat a woman are just two of the practices that have set me apart and helped me to succeed, and I know they will work for you, too.

In this book I've focused on ways you can personalize your wedding and help your fiancée create a statement of your own style for your family and friends. But just as important, I hope you will take this information and use it after your wedding, in your new life together. Knowing how to welcome guests into your home and entertain with grace and style are techniques that can stay with you all your life and help you fill your days with friendship and laughter.

My sincerest congratulations and best wishes,

Colin

Acknowledgments

There has always been material and advice for the bride, and very little information available to the groom. I am forever grateful to all the grooms from whom I have learned so much and with whom I have shared so much laughter and joy.

A big thanks to Kathy Passero, who wrote this book with me, and to my partner, Stuart Brownstein, whose knowledge has also been imparted in its pages. I am extremely grateful for the efforts of my talented and dedicated staff in Los Angeles and New York, who do so much to make our weddings elegant and memorable. And a special thanks to my partner David Berke in Los Angeles.

Thank you to the gifted people with whom I have had the wonderful opportunity of working, and thanks for the fun we have shared over the years. Thanks to all the talented photographers who captured the images that appear in this book: Deborah Feingold, Joe Buissink, Yitzhak Dalal, Stephanie Jasper and Paul Sky from Jasper Sky, Baron Spafford, Timothy Teague, Beth Herzhaft, Alec Hemer, and Jeff and Susan Moore.

I would also like to thank my publisher, Bantam Dell Publishing Group, particularly my editors Kathleen Jayes and Diane Bartoli, and my agent, Margret McBride, from the McBride Literary Agency.

A huge thank-you to Sam Shahid, Carlos Frederico Farina, and Kelly Olsen from Shahid & Company for the very tasteful book design and for sorting through thousands and thousands of photographs.

I am forever grateful to my parents who instilled in me the importance of being a gentleman. Their teachings have guided me over the years and have allowed me to create a style of my own.

Photo Credits

Joe Buissink: Page vi, 38-39, 58, 76, 88-89, 96, 99, 100

Yitzhak Dalal: Page iv

Alison Duke: Page 84

Deborah Feingold: Page 8, 14, 36, 71, 132

Alec Hemer: Page 110, 114, 124-125

Beth Hertzhaft: Page 80

Jasper Sky Photography: Page 11, 19, 22, 29, 32, 47, 48, 53, 61, 72, 92, 106

Susan Moore/Jeff Moore/New Look Photography: Page 136-137

Baron Spafford: Page 4

David Lewis Sternfeld/Freestyle Photography: Page 62

Timothy Teague: Page 54

General Credits

Page 14: Engagement Ring: Van Cleef and Arpels

Page 19: Tabletop: Colin Cowie for Lenox Haute Couture Champagne Flutes

Page 38-39: Gown: Bob Evans, Fur: Denis Basso

Page 53: Tabletop: Colin Cowie for Lenox

Page 71: Cufflinks: Citrine and Diamond by Prince Dimitri of Yugoslavia, Suit: Calvin Klein

Page 110: Tabletop: Colin Cowie for Lenox, Au Courant

Page 114: Martini Glasses: Gucci

Page 132: Dress: Adomo Adami, Michelle Roth, NYC, Jewelry: Van Cleef and Arpels,
        Tuxedo: Calvin Klein

FOR THE GROOM

Published by Delacorte Press, Random House, Inc.

1540 Broadway, New York, New York, 10036

Delacorte Press® is a registered trademark of Random House, Inc.,
and the colophon is a trademark of Random House, Inc.

Library of Congress Cataloging-in-Publication Data is on file with the publisher

ISBN: 0-385-33443-5

Book design by Shahid & Company

Manufactured in the United States of America.
Published simultaneously in Canada.

January 2000

10 9 8 7 6 5 4 3 2

RRD

www.ColinCowie.com